A Step-by-Step Curriculum for
**Early Learners
with Autism
Spectrum Disorders**

D1556007

of related interest

How to Detect Developmental Delay and What to Do Next
Practical Interventions for Home and School
Mary Mountstephen
ISBN 978 1 84905 022 7

Understanding Applied Behavior Analysis
An Introduction to ABA for Parents, Teachers, and Other Professionals
Albert J. Kearney
Part of the JKP Essentials series
ISBN 978 1 84310 860 3

Ready, Set, Potty!
Toilet Training for Children with Autism and Other Developmental Disorders
Brenda Batts
ISBN 978 1 84905 833 9

Key Learning Skills for Children with Autism Spectrum Disorders
A Blueprint for Life
Thomas L. Whitman and Nicole DeWitt
ISBN 978 1 84905 864 3

A Step-by-Step Curriculum for
Early Learners
with Autism
Spectrum Disorders

Lindsay Hilsen, M.Ed., BCBA

Jessica Kingsley *Publishers*
London and Philadelphia

First published in 2012
by Jessica Kingsley Publishers
116 Pentonville Road
London N1 9JB, UK
and
400 Market Street, Suite 400
Philadelphia, PA 19106, USA

www.jkp.com

Library of Congress Cataloging in Publication Data
Hilsen, Lindsay.
  A step-by-step curriculum for early learners with autism spectrum disorders
/ Lindsay Hilsen.
      p. cm.
  Includes bibliographical references.
  ISBN 978-1-84905-874-2 (alk. paper)
  1. Autistic children--Education. 2. Autistic children--Education--
Curricula. 3. Children with autism spectrum disorders. 4. Behavioral
assessment. 5. Behavior therapy--Methods. 6. Behavior modification. I.
Title.
  LC4717.H55 2012
  371.94--dc23
                          2011025725

British Library Cataloguing in Publication Data
A CIP catalogue record for this book is available from the British Library

ISBN 978 1 84905 874 2
eISBN 978 0 85700 546 5

Printed and bound in the United States

This book is dedicated to my beautiful daughter
Abby and in the memory of my loving mother

Contents

Part I: Assessment

Basic Programs

Behavior Programs

Motor Programs

Receptive Programs

Expressive Programs

Action Programs

Communication Programs

Intraverbal Programs

Play Programs

Self Help Programs

Sort/Match Programs

Academic Programs

Part II: Curriculum

Basic Programs

Behavior Programs

Motor Programs

Receptive Programs

Expressive Programs

Action Programs

Communication Programs

Intraverbal Programs

Play Programs

Self Help Programs

Sort/Match Programs

Academic Programs

Part III: Mastered Programs

Basic Programs

Behavior Programs

Motor Programs

Receptive Programs

Expressive Programs

Action Programs

Communication Programs

Intraverbal Programs

Play Programs

Self Help Programs

Sort/Match Programs

Academic Programs

Acknowledgements

I would like to take this opportunity to thank all of the families that I have worked with over the past several years. Without you, I would not be where I am today. All of your children are smart and genuine; and have truly taught me so much about autism. I would also like to thank my wonderful husband Alex, my amazing father, and my sisters Staci, Melissa, and Cari for always supporting me. Last, I would like to thank you for purchasing this curriculum as by doing so you are making a big difference in the life of a child!

Introduction

This curriculum is for early learners with an autism spectrum disorder or children who could benefit from a curriculum that is based on Applied Behavior Analysis. For the purpose of this curriculum early learners refers to children that are in early intervention or in preschool. This curriculum was designed based on years of research that was conducted on best practice for children with autism. The findings of these research studies showed that Applied Behavior Analysis is one of the most promising means to teaching children with autism. For example, in 1987, Ivan Lovaas conducted a research study that showed that close to half of the children that received a program based on Applied Behavior Analysis attained a normal IQ and tested within the normal range on adaptive and social skills. Since then, many other people have replicated the same findings.

One of the more recent studies was "Early intensive behavioral treatment: Replication of the UCLA Model in a community setting," which was conducted by Cohen and colleagues in 2006. The findings of this study showed that children receiving an Applied Behavior Analysis program scored significantly higher in IQ and adaptive behavior scores than the control group. In addition, it showed that 29 percent of the group ended up being fully included in regular education without assistance and 52 percent were included with support. It is this author's opinion, based on years of proven research and years of experience in the field of autism, that Applied Behavior Analysis is the best way for children on the spectrum to learn. With that being said, the next question is: What is Applied Behavior Analysis?

"Applied Behavior Analysis (ABA) is the process of systematically applying interventions based upon the principles of learning theory to improve socially significant behaviors to a meaningful degree, and to demonstrate that the interventions employed are responsible for the improvement in behavior" (Baer, Wolf and Risley 1968; Sulzer-Azaroff and Mayer 1991). What this is saying is that ABA will take socially significant behaviors (communication, self help, fine motor, gross motor, etc.) and break each program down in a systematic way so that each child will be able to learn the skill. This is achieved through prompting, prompt fading, shaping, analyzing the data, making sure to generalize each skill to different people, settings, and with different material, and to use reinforcement to keep the child motivated and encouraged.

To keep the child encouraged and from not becoming frustrated, this curriculum suggests using errorless learning. Errorless learning is when we do not allow the child to make a mistake. If we see the child about to get the answer incorrect, we will jump in and prompt the child to ensure that they get the answer correct.

Prompting is a way to teach the child a particular skill so that the child does not get the answer incorrect. We want to provide a child with prompts for a couple of reasons. The first reason is that the child will learn the skill the correct way. Say we are teaching Johnny to clap his hands. If we say "clap hands" but Johnny touches the floor, we then just taught Johnny that "clap hands" means to touch the floor. If we say "clap hands" and then immediately prompt Johnny to clap his hands, we just taught him that the words "clap hands" and him actually clapping his hands is the correct response.

The second reason we prompt is to keep the child's motivation and self-esteem up. If we are working on a new skill and we continuously get it wrong, our motivation to perform that skill is going to go way down. In addition, we are going to become very frustrated, which will then lead to behaviors. All of this can be avoided if we use prompts and fade our prompts in a systematic manner so we do not promote prompt dependency. The most *common* prompts are provided below in a most-to-least intrusive hierarchy.

PROMPT NAME	PROMPT ABBREVIATION	PROMPT DESCRIPTION
Physical Prompt	P	You use hand over hand so there is no room for error.
Faded Physical	FP	You use more of a guide from the shoulder or elbow and lead the child to the correct answer.
Gesture	G	You point to the correct answer; you can also use your eyes to "gesture" or look at the correct answer.

The below prompts are used when you are trying to get a child to engage in verbal language. Therefore, you should not provide a verbal prompt unless you are looking for a verbal response.

PROMPT NAME	PROMPT ABBREVIATION	PROMPT DESCRIPTION
Verbal	V or VP	You provide the child with the exact word/words that you want them to say (e.g. "What is your name?—Johnny"; child then says "Johnny").
Faded Verbal	FV	You provide the child with the start of the word/words that you want them to say (e.g. "What is your name?—Joh"; child then says "Johnny").

Reinforcement is another big component of an ABA program. Think about it, there is not too much in life that we do without having some type of reinforcement involved. Whether it is getting paid at the end of the week, someone saying thank you to us, or even treating ourselves to our favorite dessert because we worked hard today. The same holds true for children on the spectrum. That is why this curriculum recommends using a reinforcement system that is appropriate for the child you are working with. It is a good idea to use a reinforcement survey every 2 weeks to see what your child finds reinforcing. It is important to note that what is reinforcing one minute may not be reinforcing the next minute. It should also be noted that what is reinforcing to one child may be aversive to another, so please do not assume that all children like Cheerios. Some ideas of reinforcers can be: food, puzzles, movie, books, game, high 5s, juice, swing, and so forth.

In regards to using reinforcers, you should always save the more preferred items for the newer programs. A child will have a tendency to need to be reinforced more often and with something more novel for a step/program they just started to work on. You may need to provide them with a highly reinforcing item on a more one-to-one basis. However, a program that the child has basically mastered will only need to be reinforced on a less frequent basis. When using reinforcement, you should always pair the actual reinforcer with behavior-specific praise. For example, "I love the way you clapped your hands, here is your juice." This is especially important because we want to make sure they understand exactly what they did to receive their reinforcer and that they learn that praise is a reinforcer in itself.

This curriculum also includes an assessment and a mastered section. The purpose of the assessment is so you can have a starting place as to what the child knows and what they need to work on. The assessment should be conducted 2–4 times throughout the year to make sure skills are being learned and that mastered programs are being retained. The mastered section is included to make sure that the child is retaining any of the skills/programs they have mastered. It is also a good idea to intersperse mastered programs with newer programs so that the child does not get frustrated and will be able to keep their self-esteem up.

When you are working on the actual curriculum section, it is recommended that either probe data be collected or trial by trial data. Probe data is a quick and easy way of seeing where the child is in terms of knowing the skill or not. Probe data is good because you are not sitting there every step of the way collecting data. A lot of people can become overwhelmed with data collection; therefore, probe data will give you the answer you are looking for, yet not spend the entire session collecting data.

Probe data can either be collected daily, weekly, bi-weekly, monthly, etc. There is no rule as to how often you collect probe data. You just want to be careful that you are not missing an opportunity to move the child up to the next step if you are not collecting data daily. For example, if you see a child 5 times a week but you only collect data every other week, that child could master some of the steps in that time frame, but you will not be able to move them up to the next step because you do not have the data to verify it. It should also be noted that just because you are not collecting data throughout the entire session does not mean that you are not teaching the skill. The same principles hold true if you want to prompt to ensure errorless learning and you want to fade your prompts so that you do not promote prompt dependency.

So the question is, how do you take probe data? The purpose of probe data is to test to see if the child has the skill the first time it is presented that day. So that is exactly when you take the data. At this point you will present the direction: if the child can do it independently then you will circle Y (yes); if the child could not do it independently then you will circle N (no). You will then move on to the next program and probe that skill. Once you are finished probing for the day, you can then put your data sheet away and just focus on teaching the skill. A skill is not considered mastered until that child receives 3 consecutive Ys (independent) in a row.

Discrete trial (trial by trial) is when you take an isolated task and present the child with a direction that indicates to them what they need to do. If the child engages in the correct behavior we will provide the child with reinforcement. This is considered 1 trial. If we present the child with the direction and the child does not respond, then we will need to prompt the child to ensure errorless learning.

When looking at a discrete trial data sheet, it will typically have 10 trials or 10 individual boxes, so that we can collect 10 single instances of data pertaining to that 1 skill. To be honest, you can use any amount of trials; however, 10 is the easiest because it is very simple to calculate the percentage of independence at the end of the day. A skill is not considered mastered until that child receives 90 percent independence over 3 consecutive sessions.

It is up to the practitioner as to which measurement procedure they would like to utilize. You can choose to just use 1 of them, or both of them; it can vary from program to program depending on the needs of the child.

For more information on ABA theory, please see Barbera and Rasmussen (2007), Kearney (2008), Newman *et al.* (2003), and Richman (2000).

About the Author

Lindsay Hilsen is a Board Certified Behavior Analyst who has dedicated her career to working with children on the autism spectrum. Mrs. Hilsen has tremendous knowledge and expertise in the field of autism and Pervasive Developmental Disorders having completed master's degrees in both special education and education. In addition, she holds New Jersey teaching certifications in special education and elementary education, and has a supervisor's certification. Mrs. Hilsen's experience in the autism field consists of being an Applied Behavior Analysis teacher for PreK– Kindergarten students in a New Jersey public school and a behavior analyst for PreK–12th grade students in another New Jersey public school, and currently she is the Autism Clinical Educator for Sunny Days Early Childhood Developmental Services, Inc., which has their headquarters in New Jersey. Mrs. Hilsen is a frequent presenter and lecturer and has spoken at events such as the Association for Behavior Analyst International's Annual Convention and at Autism New Jersey, Inc.'s Annual Convention.

Part I

Assessment

Assessment Directions

Purpose

The purpose of the assessment is to provide the carer or practitioner with a baseline of where the child is at the beginning of the program. It is recommended that the assessment be updated a minimum of twice a year.

Directions for assessment

Start with the first column in the assessment section. Write the date of the assessment in the date box. Present the child with the direction that will be stated on each program page. Then start with step 1. If the child was able to complete step 1 independently, write a + in the box. As soon as you get to a step in which the child was not able to complete on their own, write the prompt that was required in order for the child to be successful (see below). At the end of each program page, calculate the percentage of steps the child got correct. To do this you will take the number of steps the child got correct and divide it by the total number of steps. The next time you do the assessment you will be filling in the second column. Please note that, although a program may only have 6 steps, it really has 12 because you need to take into account generalization. Please remember to assess each step every time you perform the assessment. We want to make sure that, if a program was previously mastered, it is still being retained. If a skill was previously mastered according to the previous assessment and the child did not retain that skill according to the current assessment, that step/program should go back into the child's daily teaching programs.

Total percentages record sheet

Once you finish the assessment, transfer the total percentages onto the total percentages record sheet at the end of these introductory pages. Remember to fill in the date in the box that says date, and then continue down the column filling in the percentage according to the score on the assessment.

Generalization in the assessment

Generalization is included in the steps during the assessment. It is important that when we assess we look at whether the child has the skill mastered in just a one-to-one routine setting, or has it mastered in different settings, with different material, and with different people.

Prompts

This curriculum suggests that you use the prompt that will be the most successful for the child without over-prompting. So if the child is learning a brand new skill, it is probable that they will need a full physical prompt in order to be successful. However, if it is a program for which the child has an 80 percent independent rate, a gestural prompt may be all that is needed. It is also recommended that you fade prompts as quickly as possible so you do not inadvertently promote prompt dependency.

- *Physical Prompt (P)*—hand-over-hand manipulation

- *Faded Physical Prompt (FP)*—the practitioner is guiding the child

- *Gestural Prompt (G)*—the practitioner points to the correct response

- *Verbal Prompt (VP)**—the answer is verbally provided for the child

- *Faded Verbal Prompt (FV)**—the beginning part of the answer is provided for the child.

Distractors

All programs are designed to be taught in a field of 3 unless otherwise specified; 3 choices are presented to the child—1 being the targeted skill and the other 2 acting as distractors. For example, the child is working on touching the color red. The adult will lay out a picture of a red card, a blue card, and a green card. The blue and green cards will act as distractors.

---

*   A verbal/faded verbal prompt should only be used if you are requiring a verbal response.

Assessment Section Example

Child Name........................ Jonny D...............................

Quiet Hands

Teaching Procedure: Present the child with the direction: "QUIET HANDS OR HANDS DOWN."

Materials: None.

Note: Quiet hands can either be by the child's side or in front of them placed on a table.

	STEPS	date: 11/1/10	date: 2/1/11	date: 5/1/11	date: 8/1/11	date: 11/1/11
1	child will have quiet hands for 3 seconds	+	+	+	+	+
1g	generalization	+	+	+	+	+
2	child will have quiet hands for 6 seconds	P (physical prompt)	+	+	+	+
2g	generalization	P	+	+	+	+
3	child will have quiet hands for 10 seconds	P	+	+	+	+
3g	generalization	P	+	+	+	+
4	child will have quiet hands for 20 seconds	P	P	+	+	+
4g	generalization	P	P	+	+	+
5	child will have quiet hands for 30 seconds	P	P	+	+	+
5g	generalization	P	P	+	+	+
6	child will have quiet hands for 1 minute	P	P	P	+	+
6g	generalization	P	P	P	+	+
PERCENT CORRECT		16.67%	50%	83.33%	100%	100%

Choosing Programs to Work On

Once you finish the assessment section, look at the total percentage scores you have recorded (pp.25–28). Programs that received less than 90 percent should be considered a potential program. The list below is provided to help you decide which programs should be worked on first. Starter programs are all programs that should be worked on before moving to the more advanced secondary programs. It should be noted that programs are not listed in any specific order within each section.

Starter programs

Quiet Hands	Clean Up	Expressive Identification of Pictures	Says Hi
Attending	Gross Motor Imitation	Expressive Identification of Objects	Imitates Sounds
Responds to Name	Motor Imitation	Expressive Identification of Body Parts	Common Animal Intraverbals
Eye Contact	Fine Motor Imitation	Points to Communicate	Single Piece Puzzle
Pointing Program	Oral Motor Imitation	Yes/No	Shape Sorter
Responds to Various Directions to Identify an Object/Picture/ Item	One Step Directions	Manding	Plays By Self
Wait Program	Receptive Identification of Pictures	Requests with Eye Contact	Ball Play
Transition	Receptive Identification of Objects	Gets Attention of Others	Plays with Indoor Toys
Desensitization to Touch	Receptive Identification of Body Parts	Says Bye	Outdoor Play

Secondary programs

Desensitization to Dentist	Expressive Identification of Emotions	Uses Language While Playing	Match Identical Object to Object
Desensitization to Doctor	Expressive Identification of Community Helpers	Sings Songs	Match Object to Picture
Desensitization to Haircuts	Expressive Identification of Environmental Sounds	Games	Sort Identical Items
Color Between the Lines	Receptive Identification of Actions	Pretend Play	Sort Non-Identical Items
Copy Straight Lines	Expressive Identification of Actions	Drinks from a Cup	Receptive Identification of Colors
Two Step Directions	Imitates Actions of Others	Uses a Spoon	Expressive Identification of Colors
Receptive Identification of Articles of Clothing	Imitates Two Step Actions	Uses a Fork	Receptive Identification of Shapes
Receptive Identification of Familiar People	Pretends to do an Action	Getting Dressed: Shoes	Expressive Identification of Shapes
Receptive Identification of Emotions	Uses Different Words to Request	Getting Dressed: Pants	Receptive Identification of Upper Case Letters
Receptive Identification of Community Helpers	Common Intraverbals	Getting Dressed: Shirt	Expressive Identification of Lower Case Letters
Receptive Identification of Environmental Sounds	Daily Activity Intraverbals	Wash Hands	Rote Counting
Expressive Identification of Articles of Clothing	Social Questions	Dry Hands	Counting Objects
Expressive Identification of Familiar People	Various Methods of Play	Match Identical Picture to Picture	Receptive Identification of Numbers
			Expressive Identification of Numbers

Total Percentages Record Sheet

PROGRAM NAME	date:	date:	date:	date:	date:
Quiet Hands					
Attending					
Responds to Name					
Eye Contact					
Pointing Program					
Responds to Various Directions to Identify an Object/Picture/Item					
Wait Program					
Transition					
Desensitization to Touch					
Desensitization to Dentist					
Desensitization to Doctor					
Desensitization to Haircuts					
Clean Up					
Gross Motor Imitation					
Motor Imitation					
Fine Motor Imitation					
Oral Motor Imitation					
Color Between the Lines					
Copy Straight Lines					
One Step Directions					
Two Step Directions					
Receptive Identification of Pictures					
Receptive Identification of Objects					
Receptive Identification of Body Parts					
Receptive Identification of Articles of Clothing					
Receptive Identification of Familiar People					

PROGRAM NAME	date:	date:	date:	date:	date:
Receptive Identification of Emotions					
Receptive Identification of Community Helpers					
Receptive Identification of Environmental Sounds					
Expressive Identification of Pictures					
Expressive Identification of Objects					
Expressive Identification of Body Parts					
Expressive Identification of Articles of Clothing					
Expressive Identification of Familiar People					
Expressive Identification of Emotions					
Expressive Identification of Community Helpers					
Expressive Identification of Environmental Sounds					
Receptive Identification of Actions					
Expressive Identification of Actions					
Imitates Actions of Others					
Imitates Two Step Actions					
Pretends to do an Action					
Points to Communicate					
Yes/No					
Manding					
Requests with Eye Contact					
Gets Attention of Others					
Says Bye					
Says Hi					
Imitates Sounds					
Uses Different Words to Request					
Common Animal Intraverbals					

PROGRAM NAME	date:	date:	date:	date:	date:
Common Intraverbals					
Daily Activity Intraverbals					
Social Questions					
Single Piece Puzzle					
Shape Sorter					
Plays By Self					
Various Methods of Play					
Ball Play					
Plays with Indoor Toys					
Outdoor Play					
Uses Language While Playing					
Sings Songs					
Games					
Pretend Play					
Drinks from a Cup					
Uses a Spoon					
Uses a Fork					
Getting Dressed: Shoes					
Getting Dressed: Pants					
Getting Dressed: Shirt					
Wash Hands					
Dry Hands					
Match Identical Picture to Picture					
Match Identical Object to Object					
Match Object to Picture					
Sort Identical Items					
Sort Non-Identical Items					
Receptive Identification of Colors					
Expressive Identification of Colors					
Receptive Identification of Shapes					
Expressive Identification of Shapes					

PROGRAM NAME	date:	date:	date:	date:	date:
Receptive Identification of Upper Case Letters					
Receptive Identification of Lower Case Letters					
Expressive Identification of Upper Case Letters					
Expressive Identification of Lower Case Letters					
Rote Counting					
Counting Objects					
Receptive Identification of Numbers					
Expressive Identification of Numbers					

Comments

ASSESSMENT 1 COMMENTS

ASSESSMENT 2 COMMENTS

ASSESSMENT 3 COMMENTS

ASSESSMENT 4 COMMENTS

ASSESSMENT 5 COMMENTS

Basic Programs

Child Name:. . . . .

Quiet Hands

Teaching Procedure: Present the child with the direction "QUIET HANDS OR HANDS DOWN."

Materials: None.

Note: Quiet hands can either be by the child's side or in front of them placed on a table.

	STEPS	date:	date:	date:	date:	date:
1	child will have quiet hands for 3 seconds					
1g	generalization					
2	child will have quiet hands for 6 seconds					
2g	generalization					
3	child will have quiet hands for 10 seconds					
3g	generalization					
4	child will have quiet hands for 20 seconds					
4g	generalization					
5	child will have quiet hands for 30 seconds					
5g	generalization					
6	child will have quiet hands for 1 minute					
6g	generalization					
PERCENT CORRECT						

Child Name: . . . .

Attending

Teaching Procedure: Present the child with the direction "SIT QUIET." This means hands on lap/ table, feet on floor, and the child is facing the instructor. The child does not need to meet eye to eye with the instructor just as long as the child is facing the instructor and the instructor knows the child is attending.

Materials: None.

	STEPS	date:	date:	date:	date:	date:
1	child will attend within 10 seconds of the direction being presented					
1g	generalization					
2	child will attend within 5 seconds of the direction being presented					
2g	generalization					
3	child will attend within 3 seconds of the direction being presented					
3g	generalization					
PERCENT CORRECT						

Child Name: . . . .

Responds to Name

Teaching Procedure: Present the child with the direction: PRESENT CHILD'S NAME. Follow the steps below.

Materials: None.

	STEPS	date:	date:	date:	date:	date:
1	will respond to name being called within 5 seconds by looking at the person					
1g	generalization					
2	will respond to name being called within 3 seconds by looking at the person					
2g	generalization					
3	will respond to name being called within 1 second by looking at the person					
3g	generalization					
PERCENT CORRECT						

Child Name: . . . .

Eye Contact

Teaching Procedure: Present the child with the direction "LOOK AT ME."

Materials: None.

Note: Although there is a direction provided, try to not use any direction. Try to get the child to naturally look at you without adding a verbal direction.

	STEPS	date:	date:	date:	date:	date:
1	maintains eye contact for first 3 seconds					
1g	generalization					
2	maintains eye contact for first 6 seconds					
2g	generalization					
3	maintains eye contact for first 10 seconds					
3g	generalization					
PERCENT CORRECT						

Child Name:. . . . .

Pointing Program

Teaching Procedure: Present the child with the direction: "POINT TO [NAME OBJECT]" and follow steps below.

Materials: Objects/pictures that the child is familiar with.

	STEPS	date:	date:	date:	date:	date:
1	will point to item when presented immediately in front of the student within 3 seconds					
1g	generalization					
2	will point to item when presented in a down position within 3 seconds					
2g	generalization					
3	will point to item when presented on the right side position within 3 seconds					
3g	generalization					
4	will point to item when presented on the left side position within 3 seconds					
4g	generalization					
PERCENT CORRECT						

Child Name: . . . .

Responds to Various Directions to Identify an Object/Picture/Item

Teaching Procedure: Present the child with the direction: STATE THE DIRECTION IN EACH STEP.

Materials: Objects/pictures/items that the child is familiar with.

	STEPS	date:	date:	date:	date:	date:
1	child will "point to" known object/picture/item					
1g	generalization					
2	child will "touch" known object/picture/item					
2g	generalization					
3	child will "give me" known object/picture/item					
3g	generalization					
4	child will "find" known object/picture/item					
4g	generalization					
5	child will "show me" known object/picture/item					
5g	generalization					
6	child will respond to "where is the" known object/picture/item					
6g	generalization					
PERCENT CORRECT						

Behavior Programs

Child Name:. . . . .

Wait Program

Teaching Procedure: Get child to mand for an item that they want. Then tell the child "you need to wait."

Materials: Strong reinforcers.

Note: A mand is when the child communicates their wants and needs to another person *without* being asked "What do you want?" It can be in the form of a gesture, sign language, picture exchange, or words. The point of manding is to get the child to be able to walk up to another person and be able to "mand" for the item that they want. You can think of a mand as the child demanding or requesting an item.

	STEPS	date:	date:	date:	date:	date:
1	child will wait for 5 seconds before getting the requested item					
1g	generalization					
2	child will wait for 10 seconds before getting the requested item					
2g	generalization					
3	child will wait for 20 seconds before getting the requested item					
3g	generalization					
4	child will wait for 30 seconds before getting the requested item					
4g	generalization					
5	child will wait for 1 minute before getting the requested item					
5g	generalization					
6	child will wait for 3 minutes before getting the requested item					
6g	generalization					

	STEPS	date:	date:	date:	date:	date:
7	child will wait for 5 minutes before getting the requested item					
7g	generalization					
PERCENT CORRECT						

Child Name: . . . .

Transition

Teaching Procedure: Present the child with the direction: "TIME TO GO TO ____ [NAME ACTIVITY]."

Materials: None.

	STEPS	date:	date:	date:	date:	date:
1	will transition from a non-preferred activity to a preferred activity					
1g	generalization					
2	will transition from a preferred activity to a preferred activity					
2g	generalization					
3	will transition from a preferred activity to a non-preferred activity					
3g	generalization					
4	will transition from a non-preferred activity to a non-preferred activity					
4g	generalization					
PERCENT CORRECT						

Child Name:. . . . .

Desensitization to Touch

Teaching Procedure: Present the child with the direction: "GIVE ME A _____."
Materials: None.

	STEPS	date:	date:	date:	date:	date:
1	high 5					
1g	generalization					
2	pat on the back					
2g	generalization					
3	hug					
3g	generalization					
4	hold hands					
4g	generalization					
PERCENT CORRECT						

Child Name: . . . .

Desensitization to Dentist

Teaching Procedure: This program will be taught in the home for the first 3 steps, then the program will switch to actually being at the dentist office. Each step will walk you through what should be done and how.

Materials: There are children's books about going to the dentist. It is recommended that you read some of these books to your child while teaching working on this program. You will also need a toothbrush and a mirror that will fit in their mouth, then an actual dental office with a dentist.

Note: When teaching this program, use a highly reinforcing item, and as soon as they complete the task in each step, they get their reinforcer. Example: in step 4, they go to the dentist office and sit in the chair. The dentist comes in and says hi; as soon as the dentist leaves say "great job at the dentist, here is your ___ (reinforcer)."

	STEPS	date:	date:	date:	date:	date:
1	*Let's pretend we are going to the dentist. You (the child) be the dentist first;* let the child just do what they want. You can suggest things for them to do.					
1g	generalization					
2	*Let's pretend we are going to the dentist. It is my (teacher/parent) turn to be the dentist. You (child) sit in the chair and say "ah" or open mouth.*					
2g	generalization					
3	*Let's pretend we are going to the dentist. It is my (teacher/parent) turn to be the dentist. You (child) sit in the chair and say "ah" or open mouth;* then take a toothbrush and put it in their mouth for a couple of seconds. If you can, brush their teeth for a couple of seconds.					
3g	generalization					

4	*It's time to go to the dentist.* This time you will actually go to the dentist office and have the child sit in the dental chair for a couple of seconds. Then end the appointment. The dentist should not actually work on the child. They should be in the room when the child is sitting in the chair though.					
4g	generalization					
5	*It's time to go to the dentist.* Have the child sit in the dental chair and have the dentist just look in their mouth today.					
5g	generalization					
6	*It's time to go to the dentist.* Have the child sit in the dental chair and have the dentist perform the work.					
6g	generalization					
PERCENT CORRECT						

Child Name: ....

Desensitization to Doctor

Teaching Procedure: This program will be taught in the home for the first 2 steps, then the program will switch to actually being at the doctor's. Each step will walk you through what should be done and how.

Materials: Kids' doctor's kit, real doctor and doctor office.

Note: When teaching this program, use a highly reinforcing item, and as soon as they complete the task in each step, they get their reinforcer. Example: in step 3, they go to the doctor's office and sit in the exam room. The doctor comes in and says hi; as soon as the doctor leaves say "great job at the doctor, here is your ___ (reinforcer)."

	STEPS	date:	date:	date:	date:	date:
1	*Let's pretend we are going to the doctor. You (the child) be the doctor first;* let the child just do what they want. You can suggest things for them to do. Make sure you give them the kids' doctor's kit to play with.					
1g	generalization					
2	*Let's pretend we are going to the doctor. It is my (teacher / parent) turn to be the doctor.* Use the kids' doctor's kit and look in the child's ear and throat. Also listen to their chest.					
2g	generalization					
3	*It's time to go to the doctor.* This time you will actually go to the doctor office and have the child sit in the exam room. Have the doctor come in and just say hi. Then end the appointment.					
3g	generalization					
4	*It's time to go to the doctor.* This time the doctor will examine the child.					
4g	generalization					
PERCENT CORRECT						

Child Name:. . . . .

Desensitization to Haircuts

Teaching Procedure: Present the child with the direction "IT'S TIME FOR A HAIRCUT" and follow the steps below.

Materials: Play-doh scissors, smock, hair dresser, hair dresser shop.

Note: Generalization should include other people giving the haircut (until you actually get to the hair dresser, then it should be a consistent hair dresser).

	STEPS	date:	date:	date:	date:	date:
1	Tell the child. *Let's pretend to get a haircut. You (child) be the hair dresser first.* Tell the child to put a smock on you and then let the child just do what they want.					
1g	generalization					
2	*It's time for a haircut, sit down in the chair. I am going to put a smock on you.* Then just take your hand and start to touch the child's hair. End the haircut here.					
2g	generalization					
3	*It's time for a haircut, sit down in the chair. I am going to put a smock on you.* Then just take your hand and start to touch the child's hair. Then take the play-doh scissors and pretend to cut the child's hair.					
3g	generalization					

4	*It's time for a haircut, let's get in the car.* This time have the child go into the hair dresser and sit in the hair dresser's chair. Let the hair dresser just touch the child's hair and end the haircut at this point. When the child is sitting in the chair, give them something to play with or eat to help distract them. Make sure the toy/food is very reinforcing.					
4g	Generalization					
5	*It's time for a haircut, let's get in the car.* This time have the child go into the hair dresser and sit in the hair dresser's chair. Let the hair dresser just touch the child's hair first, then they can start actually cutting the hair. When the child is sitting in the chair, give them something to play with or eat to help distract them. Make sure the toy/food is very reinforcing.					
5g	generalization					
PERCENT CORRECT						

Child Name: . . . .

Clean Up

Teaching Procedure: Have the child play with toys. When finished playing, present the child with the direction "CLEAN UP."

Materials: Toys.

Note: This program is taught using backward chaining. The program can either be taught using 1 toy with many pieces (like a puzzle or Lego) or using more than 1 toy with single pieces (books).

	STEPS	date:	date:	date:	date:	date:
1	child will pick up the last piece of 1 toy/the last toy					
1g	generalization					
2	child will pick up the last 2 pieces of one toy/or the last 2 toys					
2g	generalization					
3	child will pick up the last 3 pieces of 1 toy/or the last 3 toys					
3g	generalization					
4	child will pick up the last 4 pieces of 1 toy/or the remaining 4 toys					
4g	generalization					
PERCENT CORRECT						

Motor Programs

Child Name:. . . . .

Gross Motor Imitation

Teaching Procedure: Present the child with the direction "DO THIS ___."
Materials: None.

	STEPS	date:	date:	date:	date:	date:
1	clap hands					
1g	generalization					
2	arms up					
2g	generalization					
3	stamp feet					
3g	generalization					
4	tap table					
4g	generalization					
5	arms to side					
5g	generalization					
6	pat tummy					
6g	generalization					
7	rub hands together					
7g	generalization					
8	hand on head					
8g	generalization					
9	arms out in front					
9g	generalization					
10	touch toes					
10g	generalization					
11	stomp 1 foot					
11g	generalization					
12	cross legs sitting					
12g	generalization					
13	lift and hold 1 leg					
13g	generalization					

14	place feet together					
14g	generalization					
15	spread feet apart					
15g	generalization					
16	hop					
16g	generalization					
17	lift foot and shake					
17g	generalization					
18	cross legs standing					
18g	generalization					
19	place foot forward					
19g	generalization					
20	bend side to side at waist					
20g	generalization					
21	shake head yes					
21g	generalization					
22	shake head no					
22g	generalization					
23	move head side to side					
23g	generalization					
PERCENT CORRECT						

Child Name: . . . .

Motor Imitation

Teaching Procedure: Present the child with the direction "DO THIS ___."
Materials: Car, cup, spoon, hammer, doll, drums, bowl, hat.

	STEPS	date:	date:	date:	date:	date:
1	roll car back and forth					
1g	generalization					
2	drink from a cup					
2g	generalization					
3	stir a spoon in cup					
3g	generalization					
4	bang a hammer					
4g	generalization					
5	feed doll					
5g	generalization					
6	brush hair					
6g	generalization					
7	play drums					
7g	generalization					
8	kiss a doll					
8g	generalization					
9	put object in bowl					
9g	generalization					
10	put hat on					
10g	generalization					
PERCENT CORRECT						

Child Name:. . . . .

Fine Motor Imitation

Teaching Procedure: Present the child with the direction "DO THIS ___."
Materials: None.

	STEPS	date:	date:	date:	date:	date:
1	touch thumbs together and hold					
1g	generalization					
2	touch thumb and pointer finger together					
2g	generalization					
3	bounce thumb and pointer finger					
3g	generalization					
4	spread fingers apart					
4g	generalization					
5	touch pointer fingers together					
5g	generalization					
6	touch middle fingers together					
6g	generalization					
7	touch ring fingers together					
7g	generalization					
8	touch pinky fingers together					
8g	generalization					
9	bend fingers down					
9g	generalization					
10	touch thumb and middle finger together					
10g	generalization					
PERCENT CORRECT						

Child Name: ....

Oral Motor Imitation

Teaching Procedure: Present the child with the direction "DO THIS ___."
Materials: None.

	STEPS	date:	date:	date:	date:	date:
1	open mouth					
1g	generalization					
2	open and close mouth					
2g	generalization					
3	blow (like you are blowing bubbles)					
3g	generalization					
4	lips together and blow (making raspberries with your mouth)					
4g	generalization					
5	stick your tongue out					
5g	generalization					
6	stick your tongue in and out					
6g	generalization					
PERCENT CORRECT						

Child Name: . . . .

Color Between the Lines

Teaching Procedure: Present the child with the direction "COLOR."
Materials: Crayons, paper.

	STEPS	date:	date:	date:	date:	date:
1	can color a large shape staying within the boundaries approximately 4 square inches or less					
1g	generalization					
2	can color a large shape staying within the boundaries approximately 2 square inches or less					
2g	generalization					
PERCENT CORRECT						

Child Name: . . . .

Copy Straight Lines

Teaching Procedure: Present the child with the direction "DO THIS."
Materials: Pencil or crayons, paper.

	STEPS	date:	date:	date:	date:	date:
1	can copy a straight line that is up and down					
1g	generalization					
2	can copy a straight line that is horizontal					
2g	generalization					
3	can copy a diagonal line					
3g	generalization					
4	can copy a square					
4g	generalization					
5	can copy a rectangle					
5g	generalization					
6	can copy a triangle					
6g	generalization					
PERCENT CORRECT						

Receptive Programs

Child Name: . . . .

One Step Directions

Teaching Procedure: Present the child with the direction: STATE THE DIRECTION [E.G. CLAP HANDS]. Follow the steps below.

Materials: None.

	STEPS	date:	date:	date:	date:	date:
1	clap hands					
1g	generalization					
2	stand up					
2g	generalization					
3	sit down					
3g	generalization					
4	jump					
4g	generalization					
5	wave					
5g	generalization					
6	turn around					
6g	generalization					
7	blow					
7g	generalization					
8	come here					
8g	generalization					
9	stomp feet					
9g	generalization					
10	knock					
10g	generalization					
PERCENT CORRECT						

Child Name: . . . .

Two Step Directions

Teaching Procedure: Present the child with the direction: VERBALLY STATE THE DIRECTIONS [E.G. STAND UP, GET TOY].

Materials: Toy, paper, tissue, garbage, puzzle.

	STEPS	date:	date:	date:	date:	date:
1	stand up, get toy					
1g	generalization					
2	stand up, turn around					
2g	generalization					
3	get paper, sit down					
3g	generalization					
4	get tissue, wipe your nose					
4g	generalization					
5	wipe your nose, throw out tissue					
5g	generalization					
PERCENT CORRECT						

Child Name:. . . . .

Receptive Identification of Pictures

Teaching Procedure: Present the child with the direction "TOUCH/POINT TO/SHOW ME ___ [NAME PICTURE]."

Materials: Pictures presented in the steps below.

Note: Generalization should include pointing to pictures in books or magazines.

	STEPS	date:	date:	date:	date:	date:
1	table					
1g	generalization					
2	chair					
2g	generalization					
3	door					
3g	generalization					
4	sink					
4g	generalization					
5	toilet					
5g	generalization					
6	spoon					
6g	generalization					
7	plate					
7g	generalization					
8	book					
8g	generalization					
9	toy					
9g	generalization					
10	crayon					
10g	generalization					
11	paper					
11g	generalization					
12	computer					

12g	generalization					
13	window					
13g	generalization					
14	teddy bear					
14g	generalization					
15	candy					
15g	generalization					
16	camera					
16g	generalization					
17	phone					
17g	generalization					
18	sock					
18g	generalization					
19	shoe					
19g	generalization					
PERCENT CORRECT						

Child Name:. . . . .

Receptive Identification of Objects

Teaching Procedure: Present the child with the direction "TOUCH/POINT TO/SHOW ME _____ [NAME OBJECT]."

Materials: Objects presented in the steps below.

	STEPS	date:	date:	date:	date:	date:
1	sock					
1g	generalization					
2	shoe					
2g	generalization					
3	pencil					
3g	generalization					
4	paper					
4g	generalization					
5	crayon					
5g	generalization					
6	cup					
6g	generalization					
7	camera					
7g	generalization					
8	phone					
8g	generalization					
9	television					
9g	generalization					
10	door					
10g	generalization					
11	toilet					
11g	generalization					
12	sink					
12g	generalization					

13	book					
13g	generalization					
14	balloons					
14g	generalization					
15	table					
15g	generalization					
16	chair					
16g	generalization					
17	teddy bear					
17g	generalization					
18	candy					
18g	generalization					
19	blocks					
19g	generalization					
PERCENT CORRECT						

Child Name:. . . . .

Receptive Identification of Body Parts

Teaching Procedure: Present the child with the direction "TOUCH ____ [BODY PART]."

Materials: Dolls, pictures.

Note: Generalization of this program should be touching body parts on other items: other people, dolls, pictures, etc.

	STEPS	date:	date:	date:	date:	date:
1	nose					
1g	generalization					
2	eyes					
2g	generalization					
3	ears					
3g	generalization					
4	mouth					
4g	generalization					
5	arm					
5g	generalization					
6	leg					
6g	generalization					
7	foot					
7g	generalization					
8	hand					
8g	generalization					
9	elbow					
9g	generalization					
10	knee					
10g	generalization					
11	chin					
11g	generalization					
12	head					

12g	generalization					
13	hair					
13g	generalization					
14	back					
14g	generalization					
15	stomach					
15g	generalization					
16	forehead					
16g	generalization					
17	neck					
17g	generalization					
18	tongue					
18g	generalization					
PERCENT CORRECT						

Child Name: . . . .

Receptive Identification of Articles of Clothing

Teaching Procedure: In a field of 3 or more, lay out the articles of clothing and ask the child to "TOUCH/POINT/SHOW ME _____ [NAME ARTICLE OF CLOTHING]."

Materials: Various articles of clothing including pictures of clothing and actual articles of clothing.

Note: Generalization should include identifying articles of clothing on self and other people, in books, and on dolls.

	STEPS	date:	date:	date:	date:	date:
1	shirt					
1g	generalization					
2	pants					
2g	generalization					
3	socks					
3g	generalization					
4	shoes					
4g	generalization					
5	underwear/diaper					
5g	generalization					
6	shorts					
6g	generalization					
7	jacket					
7g	generalization					
8	hat					
8g	generalization					
9	gloves					
9g	generalization					
PERCENT CORRECT						

Child Name: . . . .

Receptive Identification of Familiar People

Teaching Procedure: Present the child with the direction "SHOW ME ___ [NAME THE PERSON]."

Materials: Pictures of people stated below.

Note: Generalization should be actual person and other pictures of the person, in addition to be presented with the picture in different settings and with different people.

	STEPS	date:	date:	date:	date:	date:
1	mom					
1g	generalization					
2	dad					
2g	generalization					
3	sibling					
3g	generalization					
4	grandmother					
4g	generalization					
5	teacher					
5g	generalization					
6	friend					
6g	generalization					
PERCENT CORRECT						

Child Name:...

Receptive Identification of Emotions

Teaching Procedure: Present the child with the direction "TOUCH ____ [NAME THE EMOTION]."

Materials: Picture cards of the emotions. You can obtain picture cards of emotions through the websites www.do2learn.com and www.difflearn.com. You can also take pictures of yourself demonstrating different emotions.

Note: Generalization should include identifying emotions through pictures, television, books, magazines, and on people.

	STEPS	date:	date:	date:	date:	date:
1	happy					
1g	generalization					
2	sad					
2g	generalization					
3	angry/mad					
3g	generalization					
4	surprised					
4g	generalization					
5	scared					
5g	generalization					
6	bored					
6g	generalization					
7	embarrassed					
7g	generalization					
PERCENT CORRECT						

Child Name: . . . .

Receptive Identification of Community Helpers

Teaching Procedure: Present the child with the direction "SHOW ME/POINT TO/TOUCH _____ [COMMUNITY HELPER]."

Materials: Pictures of items below.

	STEPS	date:	date:	date:	date:	date:
1	policeman					
1g	generalization					
2	fireman					
2g	generalization					
3	mail man					
3g	generalization					
4	doctor					
4g	generalization					
5	nurse					
5g	generalization					
6	bus driver					
6g	generalization					
7	waiter					
7g	generalization					
8	teacher					
8g	generalization					
PERCENT CORRECT						

Child Name:. . . . .

Receptive Identification of Environmental Sounds

Teaching Procedure: Present the child with the direction "WHAT SOUND DO YOU HEAR?"
[CHILD WILL POINT/TOUCH THE CORRECT SOUND].

Materials: Sounds of steps below, pictures of steps below.

	STEPS	date:	date:	date:	date:	date:
1	dog					
1g	generalization					
2	fire truck					
2g	generalization					
3	train					
3g	generalization					
4	horn (on car)					
4g	generalization					
5	airplane					
5g	generalization					
6	ambulance					
6g	generalization					
7	bird					
7g	generalization					
8	telephone ringing					
8g	generalization					
9	door bell					
9g	generalization					
10	baby crying					
10g	generalization					
PERCENT CORRECT						

Expressive Programs

Child Name:. . . . .

Expressive Identification of Pictures

Teaching Procedure: Present the child with the diretion "WHAT IS THIS? _____ [WHILE HOLDING UP PICTURE/POINTING TO PICTURE]."

Materials: Objects presented in the steps below.

	STEPS	date:	date:	date:	date:	date:
1	table					
1g	generalization					
2	chair					
2g	generalization					
3	door					
3g	generalization					
4	sink					
4g	generalization					
5	toilet					
5g	generalization					
6	spoon					
6g	generalization					
7	plate					
7g	generalization					
8	book					
8g	generalization					
9	toy					
9g	generalization					
10	crayon					
10g	generalization					
11	paper					
11g	generalization					
12	computer					
12g	generalization					

13	window					
13g	generalization					
14	teddy bear					
14g	generalization					
15	candy					
15g	generalization					
16	camera					
16g	generalization					
17	phone					
17g	generalization					
18	sock					
18g	generalization					
19	shoe					
19g	generalization					
PERCENT CORRECT						

Child Name: . . . .

Expressive Identification of Objects

Teaching Procedure: Present the child with the direction "WHAT IS THIS? _____ [WHILE HOLDING UP OBJECT/POINTING TO OBJECT]."

Materials: Objects presented in the steps below.

	STEPS	date:	date:	date:	date:	date:
1	sock					
1g	generalization					
2	shoe					
2g	generalization					
3	pencil					
3g	generalization					
4	paper					
4g	generalization					
5	crayon					
5g	generalization					
6	cup					
6g	generalization					
7	camera					
7g	generalization					
8	phone					
8g	generalization					
9	television					
9g	generalization					
10	door					
10g	generalization					
11	toilet					
11g	generalization					
12	sink					
12g	generalization					

13	book					
13g	generalization					
14	balloons					
14g	generalization					
15	table					
15g	generalization					
16	chair					
16g	generalization					
17	teddy bear					
17g	generalization					
18	candy					
18g	generalization					
19	blocks					
19g	generalization					
PERCENT CORRECT						

Child Name:. . . . .

Expressive Identification of Body Parts

Teaching Procedure: Present the child with the direction: POINT TO A BODY PART AND ASK CHILD TO NAME IT.

Materials: Dolls, pictures.

Note: Generalization of this program should be labeling body parts on other items: other people, dolls, pictures, etc.

	STEPS	date:	date:	date:	date:	date:
1	nose					
1g	generalization					
2	eyes					
2g	generalization					
3	ears					
3g	generalization					
4	mouth					
4g	generalization					
5	arm					
5g	generalization					
6	leg					
6g	generalization					
7	foot					
7g	generalization					
8	hand					
8g	generalization					
9	elbow					
9g	generalization					
10	knee					
10g	generalization					
11	chin					
11g	generalization					
12	head					

12g	generalization					
13	hair					
13g	generalization					
14	back					
14g	generalization					
15	stomach					
15g	generalization					
16	forehead					
16g	generalization					
17	neck					
17g	generalization					
18	tongue					
18g	generalization					
PERCENT CORRECT						

Child Name: ....

Expressive Identification of Articles of Clothing

Teaching Procedure: Hold up the article of clothing and ask the child "WHAT IS IT?" Generalization should include identifying the clothing on self and on others.

Materials: Various articles of clothing.

	STEPS	date:	date:	date:	date:	date:
1	shirt					
1g	generalization					
2	pants					
2g	generalization					
3	socks					
3g	generalization					
4	shoes					
4g	generalization					
5	underwear/diaper					
5g	generalization					
6	shorts					
6g	generalization					
7	jacket					
7g	generalization					
8	hat					
8g	generalization					
9	gloves					
9g	generalization					
PERCENT CORRECT						

Child Name: . . . .

Expressive Identification of Familiar People

Teaching Procedure: Present the child with the direction "WHO IS THIS? _____ [WHILE HOLDING UP PICTURE]."

Materials: Pictures of people stated below.

Note: Generalization should be actual person and other pictures of the person, in addition to presenting the child with the picture in different settings and with different people.

	STEPS	date:	date:	date:	date:	date:
1	mom					
1g	generalization					
2	dad					
2g	generalization					
3	sibling					
3g	generalization					
4	grandmother					
4g	generalization					
5	teacher					
5g	generalization					
6	friend					
6g	generalization					
PERCENT CORRECT						

Child Name:..

Expressive Identification of Emotions

Teaching Procedure: Direction: "HOW ITS THE PERSON FEELING?"

Materials: Picture cards of the emotions. You can obtain picture cards of emotions through the websites www.do2learn.com and www.difflearn.com. You can also take pictures of yourself demonstrating different emotions.

Note: Generalization should be actual people acting out the emotion which can include television.

	STEPS	date:	date:	date:	date:	date:
1	happy					
1g	generalization					
2	sad					
2g	generalization					
3	angry/mad					
3g	generalization					
4	surprised					
4g	generalization					
5	scared					
5g	generalization					
6	bored					
6g	generalization					
7	embarrassed					
7g	generalization					
PERCENT CORRECT						

Child Name: . . . .

Expressive Identification of Community Helpers

Teaching Procedure: Present the child with the direction "WHO IS THIS PERSON? _____ [WHILE HOLDING UP PICTURE/POINTING TO PICTURE]."

Materials: Pictures presented in the steps below.

Note: Generalization should try to include the child identifying an actual community helper, and not just through pictures.

	STEPS	date:	date:	date:	date:	date:
1	policeman					
1g	generalization					
2	fireman					
2g	generalization					
3	mail man					
3g	generalization					
4	doctor					
4g	generalization					
5	nurse					
5g	generalization					
6	bus driver					
6g	generalization					
7	waiter					
7g	generalization					
PERCENT CORRECT						

Child Name: . . . .

Expressive Identification of Environmental Sounds

Teaching Procedure: Present the child with the direction: "WHAT SOUND DO YOU HEAR?"

Materials: Sounds of a dog barking, a fire truck siren, a train whistle, a horn, an airplane, an ambulance siren, a bird chirping, a telephone ringing, a door bell, a baby crying.

	STEPS	date:	date:	date:	date:	date:
1	dog					
1g	generalization					
2	fire truck					
2g	generalization					
3	train					
3g	generalization					
4	horn (on car)					
4g	generalization					
5	airplane					
5g	generalization					
6	ambulance					
6g	generalization					
7	bird					
7g	generalization					
8	telephone ringing					
8g	generalization					
9	door bell					
9g	generalization					
10	baby crying					
10g	generalization					
PERCENT CORRECT						

Action Programs

Child Name:. . . . .

Receptive Identification of Actions

Teaching Procedure: Present the child with the direction "SHOW ME/POINT TO/TOUCH _____ [ACTION]."

Materials: Pictures of items below.

	STEPS	date:	date:	date:	date:	date:
1	jumping					
1g	generalization					
2	hopping					
2g	generalization					
3	walking					
3g	generalization					
4	sleeping					
4g	generalization					
5	hugging					
5g	generalization					
6	sitting					
6g	generalization					
7	drinking					
7g	generalization					
8	eating					
8g	generalization					
9	falling					
9g	generalization					
10	playing					
10g	generalization					
11	cutting					
11g	generalization					
12	crying					
12g	generalization					

13	brushing					
13g	generalization					
14	blowing					
14g	generalization					
15	dancing					
15g	generalization					
16	crawling					
16g	generalization					
17	reading					
17g	generalization					
18	drawing					
18g	generalization					
PERCENT CORRECT						

Child Name: . . . .

Expressive Identification of Actions

Teaching Procedure: Present the child with the direction "WHAT IS THE PERSON DOING? _____ [WHILE HOLDING UP PICTURE/POINTING TO PICTURE]."

Materials: Pictures presented in the steps below.

Note: Generalization should include an actual person acting out the action with the direction "What am I doing?"

	STEPS	date:	date:	date:	date:	date:
1	jumping					
1g	generalization					
2	hopping					
2g	generalization					
3	walking					
3g	generalization					
4	sleeping					
4g	generalization					
5	hugging					
5g	generalization					
6	sitting					
6g	generalization					
7	drinking					
7g	generalization					
8	eating					
8g	generalization					
9	falling					
9g	generalization					
10	playing					
10g	generalization					
11	cutting					
11g	generalization					
12	crying					

12g	generalization					
13	brushing					
13g	generalization					
14	blowing					
14g	generalization					
15	dancing					
15g	generalization					
16	crawling					
16g	generalization					
17	reading					
17g	generalization					
18	drawing					
18g	generalization					
PERCENT CORRECT						

Child Name:. . . . .

Imitates Actions of Others

Teaching Procedure: Start to do the action while making sure the child is attending. Do not ask the child to do what you are doing, or to look at you. The purpose of this program is for the child to start to naturally pick up on what you/others are doing and just imitate them.

Materials: None.

	STEPS	date:	date:	date:	date:	date:
1	clap hands					
1g	generalization					
2	stamp feet					
2g	generalization					
3	jump					
3g	generalization					
4	sit down					
4g	generalization					
5	stand up					
5g	generalization					
PERCENT CORRECT						

Child Name: . . . .

Imitates Two Step Actions

Teaching Procedure: Present the child with the direction "DO THIS ___."
Materials: None.

	STEPS	date:	date:	date:	date:	date:
1	clap hands, tap thighs (after model has finished)					
1g	generalization					
2	stand up, turn around (after model has finished)					
2g	generalization					
3	tap table, wave (after model has finished)					
3g	generalization					
4	arms up, arms on hips (after model has finished)					
4g	generalization					
5	touch head, hands on shoulders (after model has finished)					
5g	generalization					
6	stamp feet, clap hands (after model has finished)					
6g	generalization					
7	feet together, feet apart (after model has finished)					
7g	generalization					
8	rub tummy, open mouth (after model has finished)					
8g	generalization					
9	open and close mouth, wave (after model has finished)					
9g	generalization					
10	jump, sit down (after model has finished)					
10g	generalization					
	PERCENT CORRECT					

Child Name: . . . .

Pretends to do an Action

Teaching Procedure: Present the child with the direction "SHOW ME HOW YOU _____ [NAME ACTION]."

Materials: Dolls, pictures, actual articles of clothing.

Note: This program differs from expressive action identification in that the child is the one acting out the action.

	STEPS	date:	date:	date:	date:	date:
1	laughing					
1g	generalization					
2	crying					
2g	generalization					
3	sleeping					
3g	generalization					
4	writing					
4g	generalization					
5	cutting					
5g	generalization					
6	jumping					
6g	generalization					
7	dancing					
7g	generalization					
8	reading					
8g	generalization					
9	eating					
9g	generalization					
10	drinking					
10g	generalization					
PERCENT CORRECT						

Communication Programs

Child Name:. . . . .

Points to Communicate

Teaching Procedure: Present the child with the direction "SHOW ME WHAT YOU WANT."

Materials: Preferred objects that the child would want.

	STEPS	date:	date:	date:	date:	date:
1	hold up reinforcing object and present direction					
1g	generalization					
2	hold up 2 reinforcing objects and present direction					
2g	generalization					
3	child will point to desired object in a field of 3 when presented with direction					
3g	generalization					
4	child will point to any known item when asked to find it					
4g	generalization					
5	child will show you what they want by pointing to it					
5g	generalization					
PERCENT CORRECT						

Child Name: . . . .

Yes/No

Teaching Procedure: Present the child with the direction "DO YOU WANT THIS ___?"

Materials: Preferred and non-preferred items.

Note: To identify a preferred item, allow the child to get up and play with what he or she wants. After 2–3 seconds of play, take item away and present the direction "Do you want this?" To make sure there is no confusion for non-preferred items, use something that is not a toy or a potential reinforcer.

	STEPS	date:	date:	date:	date:	date:
1	present the child with a preferred item and present direction					
1g	generalization					
2	present the child with a non-preferred item and present direction					
2g	generalization					
3	randomly present preferred and non-preferred items					
3g	generalization					
PERCENT CORRECT						

Child Name:. . . . .

Manding

Teaching Procedure: Present the child with situations in which they would need to mand for the item/object/etc. (see steps below). If you provide them with the visual it is considered a prompted mand.

Materials: None.

Note: A mand is when the child communicates their wants and needs to another person *without* being asked "What do you want?" It can be in the form of a gesture, sign language, picture exchange, or words. The point of manding is to get the child to be able to walk up to another person and be able to "mand" for the item that they want. You can think of a mand as the child demanding or requesting an item.

	STEPS	date:	date:	date:	date:	date:
1	open					
1g	generalization					
2	eat					
2g	generalization					
3	drink					
3g	generalization					
4	help me					
4g	generalization					
5	sit down					
5g	generalization					
6	stand up					
6g	generalization					
7	play					
7g	generalization					
8	close					
8g	generalization					
9	all done					
9g	generalization					
PERCENT CORRECT						

Child Name: . . . .

Requests with Eye Contact

Teaching Procedure: Wait for the child to look at you before responding to their request. If the child does not look at you within 5 seconds of the request, prompt them.

Materials: None.

Note: A request can be in the form of a gesture, sign language, picture exchange, or words.

	STEPS	date:	date:	date:	date:	date:
1	looks at person for a couple of seconds at some point during the request					
1g	generalization					
2	looks at person at the start of the request					
2g	generalization					
3	looks at person at the start of the request and at the end of the request					
3g	generalization					
4	looks at person for the entire request					
4g	generalization					
PERCENT CORRECT						

Child Name:..

Gets Attention of Others

Teaching Procedure: Contrive a situation in which 1 person is busy. Tell the child to "GIVE ___ [THE BUSY PERSON] THE PIECE OF PAPER." Have the child walk over to the busy person and get their attention by either tapping their shoulder or calling their name.

Materials: None.

Note: Generalization should include using other directions than "give the paper to ___."

	STEPS	date:	date:	date:	date:	date:
1	will tap a person's shoulder to gain attention					
1g	generalization					
2	will call a person's name to gain attention					
2g	generalization					
PERCENT CORRECT						

Child Name: . . . .

Says Bye

Teaching Procedure: Direction: A PERSON LEAVING.
Materials: None.

	STEPS	date:	date:	date:	date:	date:
1	returns greeting					
1g	generalization					
2	initiates the goodbye when a person says "I am leaving"					
2g	generalization					
PERCENT CORRECT						

Child Name: . . . .

Says Hi

Teaching Procedure: Direction: THE ARRIVAL OF A PERSON.

Materials: None.

	STEPS	date:	date:	date:	date:	date:
1	says "Hi" to person first					
1g	generalization					
2	responds with "Hi" when the person says "Hi" first					
2g	generalization					
PERCENT CORRECT						

Child Name: . . . .

Imitates Sounds

Teaching Procedure: Present the child with the direction "SAY _____."
Materials: None.

	STEPS	date:	date:	date:	date:	date:
1	/a/					
1g	generalization					
2	/m/					
2g	generalization					
3	/d/					
3g	generalization					
4	/h/					
4g	generalization					
5	/p/					
5g	generalization					
6	/b/					
6g	generalization					
7	/t/					
7g	generalization					
8	/g/					
8g	generalization					
9	/n/					
9g	generalization					
	PERCENT CORRECT					

Child Name:. . . . .

Uses Different Words to Request

Teaching Procedure: This program should be taught with reinforcing items. Present the reinforcing item and follow the steps below. The direction is the presence of the reinforcing item.

Materials: Highly motivating items that the child will want to request.

	STEPS	date:	date:	date:	date:	date:
1	I want					
1g	generalization					
2	Can I have					
2g	generalization					
3	Give me please					
3g	generalization					
4	I need					
4g	generalization					
PERCENT CORRECT						

Intraverbal Programs

Child Name: . . . .

Common Animal Intraverbals

Teaching Procedure: Present the child with the direction "A _____ [FILL IN ANIMAL] SAYS _____."
Materials: None.

	STEPS	date:	date:	date:	date:	date:
1	dog (woof or bark)					
1g	generalization					
2	cat (meow)					
2g	generalization					
3	cow (moo)					
3g	generalization					
4	pig (oink)					
4g	generalization					
5	horse (neigh)					
5g	generalization					
6	lion (roar)					
6g	generalization					
7	bear (grrrr)					
7g	generalization					
8	monkey (ooo ooo ah ah)					
8g	generalization					
9	bird (chirp)					
9g	generalization					
PERCENT CORRECT						

Child Name: . . . .

Common Intraverbals

Teaching Procedure: Present the child with the first part of the fill in and wait for the child to respond. For example in step 1: up and ___ (wait for child to say "down").

Materials: None.

	STEPS	date:	date:	date:	date:	date:
1	up and ___ (down)					
1g	generalization					
2	ready, set, ___ (go)					
2g	generalization					
3	1, 2, ___ (3)					
3g	generalization					
4	Winnie the ___ (Pooh)					
4g	generalization					
5	follow the ___ (leader)					
5g	generalization					
6	peek a ___ (boo)					
6g	generalization					
7	hide and ___ (seek)					
7g	generalization					
8	let's go ___ (play)					
8g	generalization					
9	go down the ___ (slide)					
9g	generalization					
PERCENT CORRECT						

Child Name: . . . .

Daily Activity Intraverbals

Teaching Procedure: Present the child with the question in each step. For example in step 1: "You wash your ___."

Materials: None.

	STEPS	date:	date:	date:	date:	date:
1	wash your ___ (hands)					
1g	generalization					
2	zip your ___ (jacket/coat)					
2g	generalization					
3	put on your ___ (shoes)					
3g	generalization					
4	brush your ___ (hair)					
4g	generalization					
5	sleep in a ___ (bed)					
5g	generalization					
6	you eat ___ (food)					
6g	generalization					
7	read the ___ (book)					
7g	generalization					
8	play with the ___ (toys)					
8g	generalization					
9	talk on the ___ (phone)					
9g	generalization					
PERCENT CORRECT						

Child Name: . . . .

Social Questions

Teaching Procedure: Present the child with the direction: ASK THE CHILD THE QUESTION IN EACH STEP. For example in step 1: "What is your name?"

Materials: None.

	STEPS	date:	date:	date:	date:	date:
1	name					
1g	generalization					
2	age					
2g	generalization					
3	name(s) of sibling(s)					
3g	generalization					
4	mom's name					
4g	generalization					
5	address					
5g	generalization					
6	city/town you live in					
6g	generalization					
7	state you live in					
7g	generalization					
8	telephone number					
8g	generalization					
PERCENT CORRECT						

Play Programs

Child Name:..

Single Piece Puzzle

Teaching Procedure: Present the child with the direction "DO PUZZLE."

Materials: Single piece puzzles.

Note: Use a backward chaining procedure.

	STEPS	date:	date:	date:	date:	date:
1	instructor completes all puzzle pieces EXCEPT the last 1					
1g	generalization					
2	instructor completes all puzzle pieces EXCEPT the last 2					
2g	generalization					
3	instructor completes all puzzle pieces EXCEPT the last 3					
3g	generalization					
4	instructor completes all puzzle pieces EXCEPT the last 4					
4g	generalization					
PERCENT CORRECT						

Child Name: . . . .

Shape Sorter

Teaching Procedure: Present the child with the direction "PLAY WITH SHAPE SORTER" and follow the steps below.

Materials: Shape sorter.

	STEPS	date:	date:	date:	date:	date:
1	the child will place the circle in (or whatever shape you choose)					
1g	generalization (circle)					
2	the child will place the oval in (or whatever shape you choose)					
2g	generalization (both circle and oval)					
3	the child will place the square in (or whatever shape you choose)					
3g	generalization (circle, oval, and square)					
4	the child will place the triangle in (or whatever shape you choose)					
4g	generalization (circle, oval, square, and triangle)					
5	the child will place the rectangle in (or whatever shape you choose)					
5g	generalization (circle, oval, square, triangle, and rectangle)					
6	the child will place the star in (or whatever shape you choose)					
6g	generalization (circle, oval, square, triangle, rectangle, and star)					
PERCENT CORRECT						

Child Name: . . . .

Plays By Self

Teaching Procedure: Present the child with the direction "GO PLAY."

Materials: Toys the child is able to play with by themselves.

	STEPS	date:	date:	date:	date:	date:
1	30 seconds					
1g	generalization					
2	1 minute					
2g	generalization					
3	3 minutes					
3g	generalization					
4	5 minutes					
4g	generalization					
5	up to 10 minutes					
5g	generalization					
PERCENT CORRECT						

Child Name:. . . . .

Various Methods of Play

Teaching Procedure: Present the child with the direction: STATE ACTION IN EACH STEP [E.G. BOUNCE BALL].

Materials: Various balls, various cars, brush, doll, cup, spoon, baby doll, car ramp, car tunnel, dog.

Note: Generalization should involve changing the direction to "play with [object]" and having the child demonstrate mastery of various methods of play.

	STEPS	date:	date:	date:	date:	date:
1	bounce ball					
1g	generalization					
2	roll ball					
2g	generalization					
3	throw ball					
3g	generalization					
4	kick ball					
4g	generalization					
5	make car go in a circle					
5g	generalization					
6	push car down ramp					
6g	generalization					
7	make car go through tunnel					
7g	generalization					
8	brush own hair					
8g	generalization					
9	brush doll hair					
9g	generalization					
10	brush teacher/parent hair					
10g	generalization					
11	drink from a cup					
11g	generalization					
12	pour water into a cup					

12g	generalization					
13	stir spoon in cup					
13g	generalization					
14	give baby a drink from the cup					
14g	generalization					
PERCENT CORRECT						

Child Name: ....

Ball Play

Teaching Procedure: Present the child with the direction "LET'S PLAY WITH THE BALL [THEN STATE THE ACTION YOU WANT THE CHILD TO PERFORM]." Example (step 1): "let's play with the ball, let's roll it back and forth."

Materials: Ball.

	STEPS	date:	date:	date:	date:	date:
1	roll a ball back and forth					
1g	generalization					
2	roll the ball and knock down pins					
2g	generalization					
3	kick a ball back and forth					
3g	generalization					
4	kick a ball into a goal					
4g	generalization					
5	throw a ball back and forth					
5g	generalization					
6	throw a ball at a target					
6g	generalization					
PERCENT CORRECT						

Child Name: . . . .

Plays with Indoor Toys

Teaching Procedure: Present the child with the direction "PLAY WITH ___ [TOY]."

Materials: Shape sorter, pop-up toy, puzzle, doll/action hero.

Note: Suggested toys are provided; however, use toys that are in the child's home.

	STEPS	date:	date:	date:	date:	date:
1	shape sorter					
1g	generalization					
2	pop-up toy					
2g	generalization					
3	puzzle					
3g	generalization					
4	doll/action hero					
4g	generalization					
5	cars					
5g	generalization					
PERCENT CORRECT						

Child Name: . . . .

Outdoor Play

Teaching Procedure: Present the child with the direction "PLAY WITH/ON _____."
Materials: Slide, swing, chalk, ball.

	STEPS	date:	date:	date:	date:	date:
1	goes on slide					
1g	generalization					
2	goes on swing					
2g	generalization					
3	plays with chalk					
3g	generalization					
4	plays with a ball					
4g	generalization					
PERCENT CORRECT						

Child Name: . . . .

Uses Language While Playing

Teaching Procedure: Present the child with the direction "PLAY."

Materials: Toys that the child is able to play with independently.

Note: Try to use toys like a car so the child can say "vroom"; or for a train, "choo choo."

	STEPS	date:	date:	date:	date:	date:
1	uses at least 1 word for 1 toy					
1g	generalization					
2	uses at least 2 words for 1 toy					
2g	generalization					
3	uses at least 3 words for 1 toy					
3g	generalization					
4	uses at least 3 words for 2 different toys					
4g	generalization					
5	uses at least 5 words for 3 different toys					
5g	generalization					
PERCENT CORRECT						

Child Name: . . . .

Sings Songs

Teaching Procedure: Present the child with the direction "LET'S SING _____ [NAME SONG]."
Materials: None.

	STEPS	date:	date:	date:	date:	date:
1	Itsy Bitsy Spider—hand movements only					
1a	Itsy Bitsy Spider—words if the child is verbal					
1g	generalization					
2	If You're Happy and You Know It—hand movements only					
2a	If You're Happy and You Know It—words if the child is verbal					
2g	generalization					
3	Head, Shoulder, Knees, and Toes—hand movements only					
3a	Head, Shoulder, Knees, and Toes—words if the child is verbal					
3g	generalization					
PERCENT CORRECT						

Child Name: . . . .

Games

Teaching Procedure: Present the child with the direction "LET'S PLAY ___ [NAME THE GAME]."

Materials: None.

Note: You need to teach both the words and actions with each step of duck duck goose. If the child is not verbal, then teach just the actions for both duck duck goose and ring around the rosy.

	STEPS	date:	date:	date:	date:	date:
1	duck duck goose					
1a	child sits while someone else gets picked as the goose					
1b	child is picked as the goose					
1c	child gets to be the one that walks around the circle and chooses the goose					
1g	generalization					
2	ring around the rosy					
2a	practice just the motions					
2b	learn the words					
2g	generalization					
PERCENT CORRECT						

Child Name:. . . . .

Pretend Play

Teaching Procedure: Present the child with the direction "LET'S BE A ___ [NAME CHARACTER]."
Materials: Dress-up clothes of a policeman, fireman, princess, doctor, etc.
Note: Child will need to dress up like the character and act like them too.

	STEPS	date:	date:	date:	date:	date:
1	policeman					
1g	generalization					
2	fireman					
2g	generalization					
3	doctor					
3g	generalization					
4	princess/action hero					
4g	generalization					
PERCENT CORRECT						

Self Help Programs

Child Name: . . . .

Drinks from a Cup

Teaching Procedure: Present the child with the direction "DRINK/TAKE A SIP."

Materials: Cup with highly preferred liquid in it.

	STEPS	date:	date:	date:	date:	date:
1	will pick up the cup with 2 hands					
1g	generalization					
2	will put the cup to their mouth					
2g	generalization					
3	will take 1 sip out of the cup					
3g	generalization					
4	will put the cup back down					
4g	generalization					
PERCENT CORRECT						

Child Name:. . . . .

Uses a Spoon

Teaching Procedure: Present the child with the direction "EAT."

Materials: Spoon, bowl, highly preferred edible that is easy to scoop up (yogurt, oatmeal).

	STEPS	date:	date:	date:	date:	date:
1	will pick up the spoon					
1g	generalization					
2	will take the spoon and scoop up the food					
2g	generalization					
3	will take the spoon and put it in their mouth					
3g	generalization					
4	will put the spoon down					
4g	generalization					
PERCENT CORRECT						

Child Name: . . . .

Uses a Fork

Teaching Procedure: Present the child with the direction "EAT."

Materials: Fork, highly preferred edible that is easy to stab with a fork.

	STEPS	date:	date:	date:	date:	date:
1	will pick up the fork					
1g	generalization					
2	will take the fork and stab the edible					
2g	generalization					
3	will take the fork and put it in their mouth					
3g	generalization					
4	will put the fork down					
4g	generalization					
PERCENT CORRECT						

Child Name:. . . . .

Getting Dressed: Shoes

Teaching Procedure: Present the child with the direction "PUT SHOES ON/TAKE SHOES OFF."
Materials: Shoes.
Note: Only work with Velcro shoes.

	STEPS	date:	date:	date:	date:	date:
1	can pull open the Velcro					
1g	generalization					
2	can take shoes off					
2g	generalization					
3	can put shoes on					
3g	generalization					
4	can close the Velcro					
4g	generalization					
PERCENT CORRECT						

Child Name:. . . . .

Getting Dressed: Pants

Teaching Procedure: Present the child with the direction "PUT PANTS ON/TAKE PANTS OFF."

Materials: Pants.

Note: The child does not need to zipper or button the pants.

	STEPS	date:	date:	date:	date:	date:
1	can pull pants down					
1g	generalization					
2	can pull pants down and take both feet out					
2g	generalization					
3	can pull pants up					
3g	generalization					
4	can put both feet in the pants and pull them up					
4g	generalization					
PERCENT CORRECT						

Child Name: . . . .

Getting Dressed: Shirt

Teaching Procedure: Present the child with the direction "PUT SHIRT ON/TAKE SHIRT OFF."
Materials: Shirt.

	STEPS	date:	date:	date:	date:	date:
1	can pull right arm out of sleeve					
1g	generalization					
2	can pull left arm out of sleeve					
2g	generalization					
3	can pull shirt over their head					
3g	generalization					
4	can pull shirt over their head (putting it back on)					
4g	generalization					
5	can put right arm in sleeve					
5g	generalization					
6	can put left arm in sleeve					
6g	generalization					
PERCENT CORRECT						

Child Name: . . . .

Wash Hands

Teaching Procedure: Present the child with the direction "WASH HANDS."

Materials: Sink, soap.

Note: This program should be taught using backwards chaining. This means that you will physically prompt the child through the entire sequence up until the last step. Once the last step is mastered, you will prompt the child through the sequence except the last 2 steps. This program is written so step 1 is the last step in the sequence.

	STEPS	date:	date:	date:	date:	date:
1	turn off water					
1g	generalization					
2	place both hands under the water until all soap is gone					
2g	generalization					
3	rub left palm to back of right hand					
3g	generalization					
4	rub right palm to back of left hand					
4g	generalization					
5	rub palms together					
5g	generalization					
6	get soap					
6g	generalization					
7	place hands under the water					
7g	generalization					
8	turn on cold water					
8g	generalization					
PERCENT CORRECT						

Child Name: . . . .

Dry Hands

Teaching Procedure: Present the child with the direction "DRY HANDS."

Materials: Towel.

Note: This program should be taught using backwards chaining. This means that you will physically prompt the child through the entire sequence up until the last step. Once the last step is mastered, you will prompt the child through the sequence except the last 2 steps. This program is written so step 1 is the last step in the sequence.

	STEPS	date:	date:	date:	date:	date:
1	throw out towel					
1g	generalization					
2	dry the back of the right hand					
2g	generalization					
3	dry the back of the left hand					
3g	generalization					
4	dry the palms of both hands					
4g	generalization					
5	get paper towel					
5g	generalization					
PERCENT CORRECT						

Sort/Match Programs

Child Name: . . . .

Match Identical Picture to Picture

Teaching Procedure: Present the child with the direction "MATCH" and follow the steps below.

Materials: Any common picture to picture can be used. Some suggestions are: car, animal, plate, utensils, clothing, brush, cup, book.

Note: Example of step 2 (match 2 different pictures to pictures in a field of 2). Lay down a picture of a cow and a car. Present the child with 2 pictures (1 of a cow and 1 of a car). Tell the child to match.

	STEPS	date:	date:	date:	date:	date:
1	will match a picture to picture in a field of 1					
1g	generalization—1 picture to picture in a field of 1 with 3 different people in 3 different settings					
2	will match 2 different pictures to pictures in a field of 2					
2g	generalization—up to 2 different pictures to pictures in a field of 2 with 3 different people in 3 different settings					
3	will match 3 different pictures to pictures in a field of 3					
3g	generalization—up to 3 different pictures to pictures in a field of 3 or more with 3 different people in 3 different settings					
4	will match up to 4 different pictures to pictures in a field of 3 or more					
4g	generalization—up to 4 different pictures to pictures in a field of 3 or more with 3 different people in 3 different settings					
5	will match up to 5 different pictures to pictures in a field of 3 or more					

5g	generalization—up to 5 different pictures to pictures in a field of 3 or more with 3 different people in 3 different settings					
6	will match up to 6 different pictures to pictures in a field of 3 or more					
6g	generalization—up to 6 different pictures to pictures in a field of 3 or more with 3 different people in 3 different settings					
7	will match up to 7 different pictures to pictures in a field of 3 or more					
7g	generalization—up to 7 different pictures to pictures in a field of 3 or more with 3 different people in 3 different settings					
8	will match up to 8 different pictures to pictures in a field of 3 or more					
8g	generalization—up to 8 different pictures to pictures in a field of 3 or more with 3 different people in 3 different settings					
9	will match up to 9 different pictures to pictures in a field of 3 or more					
9g	generalization—up to 9 different pictures to pictures in a field of 3 or more with 3 different people in 3 different settings					
10	will match up to 10 different pictures to pictures in a field of 3 or more					
10g	generalization—up to 10 different pictures to pictures in a field of 3 or more with 3 different people in 3 different settings					
PERCENT CORRECT						

Child Name: . . . .

Match Identical Object to Object

Teaching Procedure: Present the child with the direction "MATCH" and follow the steps below.

Materials: Any common object to object can be used. Some suggestions are: car, animal, plate, utensils, clothing, brush, cup, book.

Note: Example of step 2 (match 2 different objects to objects in a field of 2). Lay down an object of a cow and a car. Present the child with 2 objects (1 a cow and 1 a car). Tell the child to match.

	STEPS	date:	date:	date:	date:	date:
1	will match an object to object in a field of 1					
1g	generalization—1 object to object in a field of 1 with 3 different people in 3 different settings					
2	will match 2 different objects to objects in a field of 2					
2g	generalization—up to 2 different objects to objects in a field of 2 with 3 different people in 3 different settings					
3	will match 3 different objects to objects in a field of 3					
3g	generalization—up to 3 different objects to objects in a field of 3 or more with 3 different people in 3 different settings					
4	will match up to 4 different objects to objects in a field of 3 or more					
4g	generalization—up to 4 different objects to objects in a field of 3 or more with 3 different people in 3 different settings					
5	will match up to 5 different objects to objects in a field of 3 or more					

5g	generalization—up to 5 different objects to objects in a field of 3 or more with 3 different people in 3 different settings				
6	will match up to 6 different objects to objects in a field of 3 or more				
6g	generalization—up to 6 different objects to objects in a field of 3 or more with 3 different people in 3 different settings				
7	will match up to 7 different objects to objects in a field of 3 or more				
7g	generalization—up to 7 different objects to objects in a field of 3 or more with 3 different people in 3 different settings				
8	will match up to 8 different objects to objects in a field of 3 or more				
8g	generalization—up to 8 different objects to objects in a field of 3 or more with 3 different people in 3 different settings				
9	will match up to 9 different objects to objects in a field of 3 or more				
9g	generalization—up to 9 different objects to objects in a field of 3 or more with 3 different people in 3 different settings				
10	will match up to 10 different objects to objects in a field of 3 or more				
10g	generalization—up to 10 different objects to objects in a field of 3 or more with 3 different people in 3 different settings				
PERCENT CORRECT					

Child Name: . . . .

Match Object to Picture

Teaching Procedure: Present the child with the direction "MATCH" and follow the steps below.

Materials: You will need common objects that correspond to the same pictures. Some examples are: car, animal, furniture, ball, crayon, utensil, clothing.

Note: Example of step 2 (match 2 different objects to pictures in a field of 2). Lay down a picture of a cow and a car. Present the child with 2 objects (1 a cow and 1 a car). Tell the child to match.

	STEPS	date:	date:	date:	date:	date:
1	will match an object to a picture in a field of 1					
1g	generalization—1 object to a picture in a field of 1 with 3 different people in 3 different settings					
2	will match 2 different objects to pictures in a field of 2					
2g	generalization—up to 2 different objects to pictures in a field of 2 with 3 different people in 3 different settings					
3	will match 3 different objects to pictures in a field of 3					
3g	generalization—up to 3 different objects to pictures in a field of 3 or more with 3 different people in 3 different settings					
4	will match up to 4 different objects to pictures in a field of 3 or more					
4g	generalization—up to 4 different objects to pictures in a field of 3 or more with 3 different people in 3 different settings					
5	will match up to 5 different objects to pictures in a field of 3 or more					

5g	generalization—up to 5 different objects to pictures in a field of 3 or more with 3 different people in 3 different settings					
6	will match up to 6 different objects to pictures in a field of 3 or more					
6g	generalization—up to 6 different objects in a field of 3 or more with 3 different people in 3 different settings					
7	will match up to 7 different objects to pictures in a field of 3 or more					
7g	generalization—up to 7 different objects to pictures in a field of 3 or more with 3 different people in 3 different settings					
8	will match up to 8 different objects to pictures in a field of 3 or more					
8g	generalization—up to 8 different objects in a field of 3 or more with 3 different people in 3 different settings					
9	will match up to 9 different objects to pictures in a field of 3 or more					
9g	generalization—up to 9 different objects in a field of 3 or more with 3 different people in 3 different settings					
10	will match up to 10 different objects to pictures in a field of 3 or more					
10g	generalization—up to 10 different objects to pictures in a field of 3 or more with 3 different people in 3 different settings					
PERCENT CORRECT						

Child Name: . . . .

Sort Identical Items

Teaching Procedure: For steps 1–5: lay down 3 non-identical items but all from the same category (e.g. colors); give the child the matching items and ask them to sort. For example, lay down purple, red, and blue on the table. Give the child 2 purples, 2 reds, and 2 blues (at least 2) and ask them to sort. For step 6: lay down on table at least 3 different categories (clothing, utensil, shape) and give the child at least 2 items from each category and ask them to sort. For example, on the table is a shoe, fork, and square. Give the child 2 shoes, 2 forks, and 2 squares and tell them to sort.

Materials: Same exact animals, utensils, colors, shapes, clothes.

	STEPS	date:	date:	date:	date:	date:
1	in a field of 3 can sort identical colors (e.g. red to red, blue to blue, purple to purple)					
1g	generalization					
2	in a field of 3 can sort identical animals (e.g. tiger to tiger, lion to lion, dog to dog)					
2g	generalization					
3	in a field of 3 can sort identical shapes					
3g	generalization					
4	in a field of 3 can sort identical utensils					
4g	generalization					
5	in a field of 3 can sort identical articles of clothing					
5g	generalization					
6	in a field of 3 or more, sort identical items from different categories					
6g	generalization					
PERCENT CORRECT						

Child Name: . . . .

Sort Non-Identical Items

Teaching Procedure: Lay down 3 (or more, depending on the step) non-identical items: car, color, article of clothing. Present the child with 2 or more items from each category and ask them to sort. The items should be from the same category but not identical items. For example, car, blue, and shirt are on the table. Give the child 2 (or more) non-identical vehicles, 2 (or more) colors, and 2 (or more) articles of clothing and tell the child to sort.

Materials: Animals, utensils, colors, shapes, clothes, books, dolls, cars.

	STEPS	date:	date:	date:	date:	date:
1	in a field of 3 can sort non-identical items					
1g	generalization					
2	in a field of 5 can sort non-identical items					
2g	generalization					
3	in a field of 8 can sort non-identical items					
3g	generalization					
PERCENT CORRECT						

Academic Programs

Child Name:. . . . .

Receptive Identification of Colors

Teaching Procedure: In a field of 3 or more ask the child to "POINT/TOUCH/SHOW ME ____ [NAME THE COLOR]."

Materials: Various colors on different backgrounds.

	STEPS	date:	date:	date:	date:	date:
1	blue					
1g	generalization					
2	green					
2g	generalization					
3	red					
3g	generalization					
4	purple					
4g	generalization					
5	orange					
5g	generalization					
6	yellow					
6g	generalization					
7	brown					
7g	generalization					
8	black					
8g	generalization					
9	white					
9g	generalization					
10	pink					
10g	generalization					
PERCENT CORRECT						

Child Name:. . . . .

Expressive Identification of Colors

Teaching Procedure: Hold up the color and ask the child "WHAT IS IT?"
Materials: Various colors.

	STEPS	date:	date:	date:	date:	date:
1	blue					
1g	generalization					
2	green					
2g	generalization					
3	red					
3g	generalization					
4	purple					
4g	generalization					
5	orange					
5g	generalization					
6	yellow					
6g	generalization					
7	brown					
7g	generalization					
8	black					
8g	generalization					
9	white					
9g	generalization					
10	pink					
10g	generalization					
PERCENT CORRECT						

Child Name:. . . . .

Receptive Identification of Shapes

Teaching Procedure: In a field of 3 or more ask the child to "POINT/TOUCH/SHOW ME ____ [NAME THE SHAPE]."

Materials: Various shapes on different backgrounds.

	STEPS	date:	date:	date:	date:	date:
1	circle					
1g	generalization					
2	square					
2g	generalization					
3	triangle					
3g	generalization					
4	rectangle					
4g	generalization					
5	oval					
5g	generalization					
6	star					
6g	generalization					
PERCENT CORRECT						

Child Name:. . . . .

Expressive Identification of Shapes

Teaching Procedure: Hold up the shape and ask the child "WHAT SHAPE IS IT?"
Materials: Various shapes.

	STEPS	date:	date:	date:	date:	date:
1	circle					
1g	generalization					
2	square					
2g	generalization					
3	triangle					
3g	generalization					
4	rectangle					
4g	generalization					
5	oval					
5g	generalization					
6	star					
6g	generalization					
PERCENT CORRECT						

Child Name: . . . .

Receptive Identification of Upper Case Letters

Teaching Procedure: In a field of 3 or more lay out cards/pictures of individual letters, present the child with the direction "TOUCH/FIND/POINT TO ___ [LETTER]."

Materials: Various letters in different fonts and colors, and on different types of card.

	STEPS	date:	date:	date:	date:	date:
1	A					
1g	generalization					
2	B					
2g	generalization					
3	C					
3g	generalization					
4	D					
4g	generalization					
5	E					
5g	generalization					
6	F					
6g	generalization					
7	G					
7g	generalization					
8	H					
8g	generalization					
9	I					
9g	generalization					
10	J					
10g	generalization					
11	K					
11g	generalization					
12	L					
12g	generalization					

13	M					
13g	generalization					
14	N					
14g	generalization					
15	O					
15g	generalization					
16	P					
16g	generalization					
17	Q					
17g	generalization					
18	R					
18g	generalization					
19	S					
19g	generalization					
20	T					
20g	generalization					
21	U					
21g	generalization					
22	V					
22g	generalization					
23	W					
23g	generalization					
24	X					
24g	generalization					
25	Y					
25g	generalization					
26	Z					
26g	generalization					
PERCENT CORRECT						

Child Name:..

Receptive Identification of Lower Case Letters

Teaching Procedure: In a field of 3 or more lay out cards/pictures of individual letters; present the child with the direction "TOUCH/FIND/POINT TO ___ [LETTER]."

Materials: Various letters in different fonts and colors, and on different types of card.

	STEPS	date:	date:	date:	date:	date:
1	a					
1g	generalization					
2	b					
2g	generalization					
3	c					
3g	generalization					
4	d					
4g	generalization					
5	e					
5g	generalization					
6	f					
6g	generalization					
7	g					
7g	generalization					
8	h					
8g	generalization					
9	i					
9g	generalization					
10	j					
10g	generalization					
11	k					
11g	generalization					
12	l					
12g	generalization					

13	m					
13g	generalization					
14	n					
14g	generalization					
15	o					
15g	generalization					
16	p					
16g	generalization					
17	q					
17g	generalization					
18	r					
18g	generalization					
19	s					
19g	generalization					
20	t					
20g	generalization					
21	u					
21g	generalization					
22	v					
22g	generalization					
23	w					
23g	generalization					
24	x					
24g	generalization					
25	y					
25g	generalization					
26	z					
26g	generalization					
PERCENT CORRECT						

Child Name:. . . . .

Expressive Identification of Upper Case Letters

Teaching Procedure: Hold up the letter and ask the child "WHAT LETTER IS IT?"

Materials: Various letters in different fonts and colors, and on different types of card.

	STEPS	date:	date:	date:	date:	date:
1	A					
1g	generalization					
2	B					
2g	generalization					
3	C					
3g	generalization					
4	D					
4g	generalization					
5	E					
5g	generalization					
6	F					
6g	generalization					
7	G					
7g	generalization					
8	H					
8g	generalization					
9	I					
9g	generalization					
10	J					
10g	generalization					
11	K					
11g	generalization					
12	L					
12g	generalization					
13	M					

13g	generalization					
14	N					
14g	generalization					
15	O					
15g	generalization					
16	P					
16g	generalization					
17	Q					
17g	generalization					
18	R					
18g	generalization					
19	S					
19g	generalization					
20	T					
20g	generalization					
21	U					
21g	generalization					
22	V					
22g	generalization					
23	W					
23g	generalization					
24	X					
24g	generalization					
25	Y					
25g	generalization					
26	Z					
26g	generalization					
PERCENT CORRECT						

Child Name:..

Expressive Identification of Lower Case Letters

Teaching Procedure: Hold up the letter and ask the child "WHAT LETTER IS IT?"

Materials: Various letters in different fonts and colors, and on different types of card.

	STEPS	date:	date:	date:	date:	date:
1	a					
1g	generalization					
2	b					
2g	generalization					
3	c					
3g	generalization					
4	d					
4g	generalization					
5	e					
5g	generalization					
6	f					
6g	generalization					
7	g					
7g	generalization					
8	h					
8g	generalization					
9	i					
9g	generalization					
10	j					
10g	generalization					
11	k					
11g	generalization					
12	l					
12g	generalization					
13	m					

13g	generalization					
14	n					
14g	generalization					
15	o					
15g	generalization					
16	p					
16g	generalization					
17	q					
17g	generalization					
18	r					
18g	generalization					
19	s					
19g	generalization					
20	t					
20g	generalization					
21	u					
21g	generalization					
22	v					
22g	generalization					
23	w					
23g	generalization					
24	x					
24g	generalization					
25	y					
25g	generalization					
26	z					
26g	generalization					
PERCENT CORRECT						

Child Name:. . . . .

Rote Counting

Teaching Procedure: Present the child with the direction "COUNT TO ___ [NAME THE NUMBER]."

Materials: None.

	STEPS	date:	date:	date:	date:	date:
1	can count to 5					
1g	generalization					
2	can count to 10					
2g	generalization					
3	can count to 15					
3g	generalization					
4	can count to 20					
4g	generalization					
5	can count to 25					
5g	generalization					
6	can count to 30					
6g	generalization					
PERCENT CORRECT						

Child Name: . . . .

Counting Objects

Teaching Procedure: Present the child with the direction "COUNT."

Materials: Various objects that can be counted.

	STEPS	date:	date:	date:	date:	date:
1	can count objects up to 2					
1g	generalization					
2	can count objects up to 3					
2g	generalization					
3	can count objects up to 4					
3g	generalization					
4	can count objects up to 5					
4g	generalization					
5	can count objects up to 6					
5g	generalization					
6	can count objects up to 7					
6g	generalization					
7	can count objects up to 8					
7g	generalization					
8	can count objects up to 9					
8g	generalization					
9	can count objects up to 10					
9g	generalization					
PERCENT CORRECT						

Child Name: . . . .

Receptive Identification of Numbers

Teaching Procedure: In a field of 3 or more present the child with the direction "SHOW ME/POINT TO/TOUCH ___ [NAME THE NUMBER]."

Materials: Cards with numbers on them (use different cards for generalization).

	STEPS	date:	date:	date:	date:	date:
1	1					
1g	generalization					
2	2					
2g	generalization					
3	3					
3g	generalization					
4	4					
4g	generalization					
5	5					
5g	generalization					
6	6					
6g	generalization					
7	7					
7g	generalization					
8	8					
8g	generalization					
9	9					
9g	generalization					
10	10					
10g	generalization					
11	11					
11g	generalization					
12	12					
12g	generalization					

13	13					
13g	generalization					
14	14					
14g	generalization					
15	15					
15g	generalization					
16	16					
16g	generalization					
17	17					
17g	generalization					
18	18					
18g	generalization					
19	19					
19g	generalization					
20	20					
20g	generalization					
PERCENT CORRECT						

Child Name: ....

Expressive Identification of Numbers

Teaching Procedure: Hold up the number and ask the child "WHAT NUMBER IS IT?"

Materials: Cards with numbers on them (use different cards for generalization).

	STEPS	date:	date:	date:	date:	date:
1	1					
1g	generalization					
2	2					
2g	generalization					
3	3					
3g	generalization					
4	4					
4g	generalization					
5	5					
5g	generalization					
6	6					
6g	generalization					
7	7					
7g	generalization					
8	8					
8g	generalization					
9	9					
9g	generalization					
10	10					
10g	generalization					
11	11					
11g	generalization					
12	12					
12g	generalization					
13	13					

13g	generalization					
14	14					
14g	generalization					
15	15					
15g	generalization					
16	16					
16g	generalization					
17	17					
17g	generalization					
18	18					
18g	generalization					
19	19					
19g	generalization					
20	20					
20g	generalization					
PERCENT CORRECT						

Part II

Curriculum

Curriculum Directions

Purpose

This curriculum is intended for therapists and/or parents (the adults) who work with early learners with an autism spectrum disorder or who learn through a behavioral approach. The curriculum is designed to provide the adult with the framework so that working with the child becomes much easier. A task analysis was developed for each program so that data can be analyzed along the way to make sure the child is progressing. It also allows the child to be more successful because the program is broken down into achievable steps. On each program page, make sure you document when the program (and individual step) started and when the child mastered them.

Assessment

The assessment at the beginning of the curriculum is provided so the practitioner can develop goals and have an ongoing tracking system to show the child's progress. It is recommended that the assessment be updated a minimum of twice a year.

Mastered section

The mastered forms in this curriculum are provided so that continued documentation can be collected on skills the child has mastered. The mastered skills are designed to use probe data collection.

Measurement

A specific measurement procedure is not provided. It is recommended that either probe data be collected or trial by trial data. It is up to the practitioner or parent which measurement procedure they would like to utilize. This can vary from program to program.

Criterion

A specific criterion is not provided. It is recommended that the criterion be either 3 consecutive independents (Y) if you are using probe as your measurement procedure or 90 percent independent over 3 consecutive days if you are using trial by trial as your measurement. If the child's data shows a decreasing trend or no trend at all after 5 consecutive days, the program should be discontinued or tweaked.

Prompts

This curriculum (as with the assessment section) suggests that you use the prompt that will be the most successful for the child without over-prompting. So if the child is learning a brand new skill, it is probable that they will need a full physical prompt in order to be successful. However, if it is a program that the child has an 80 percent independent rate, a gestural prompt may be all that is needed. It is also recommended that you fade prompts as quickly as possible so you do not inadvertently promote prompt dependency.

- *Physical Prompt (P)*—hand-over-hand manipulation

- *Faded Physical Prompt (FP)*—the practitioner is guiding the child

- *Gestural Prompt (G)*—the practitioner points to the correct response

- *Verbal Prompt (VP)**—the answer is verbally provided for the child

- *Faded Verbal Prompt (FV)**—the beginning part of the answer is provided for the child.

Errorless learning

It is recommended that you implement this curriculum using errorless learning. An example is provided below:

Present direction—no response/incorrect response—immediately prompt using the least intrusive prompt that will ensure that the child gets the answer correct—immediately represent the direction—immediately prompt. This counts as one trial.

Distractors

All programs are designed to be taught in a field of 3 unless otherwise specified; 3 choices are presented to the child—1 being the targeted skill and the other 2 acting as distractors. For example, the child is working on touching the color red. The adult will lay out a picture of a red card, a blue card, and a green card. The blue and green cards will act as distractors.

Generalization

Each program has generalization built into the task analysis. Generalization means that the step the child is on should be taught in at least 3 different settings, with at least 3 different materials, and with at least 3 different people. Generalization of different people can include but should not be limited to: parents, grandparents, siblings, friends, teachers, people in the community. Generalization of different settings can include but should not be limited to:

---

different rooms in the house, mall, playground, school, restaurant, someone else's home. Generalization of different materials can include but should not be limited to: different puzzles, different books, using magazines, using movies, using the television, using different dolls, using real kitchen utensils, etc.

Curriculum Section Example

Child Name: . . . . Johnny D. . . . .

Quiet Hands

Teaching Procedure: Present the child with the direction "QUIET HANDS OR HANDS DOWN."

Prompt Hierarchy: Use the least intrusive prompt required in order for the child to be successful (no prompt, gestural, faded physical, physical).

Materials: None.

Note: Quiet hands can either be by the child's side or in front of them placed on a table.

program started: 11/1/10		program mastered: 6/13/11		
	STEPS	**STARTED**	**MASTERED**	**COMMENTS**
1	child will have quiet hands for 3 seconds			Mastered according to 11/1/10 assessment
1g	generalization			Mastered according to 11/1/10 assessment
2	child will have quiet hands for 6 seconds	11/1/10	11/27/10	
2g	generalization	12/5/10	12/15/10	
3	child will have quiet hands for 10 seconds	12/18/10	1/23/11	
3g	generalization	1/25/11	1/29/11	
4	child will have quiet hands for 20 seconds	2/5/11	3/1/11	
4g	generalization	3/3/11	3/16/11	
5	child will have quiet hands for 30 seconds	3/20/11	4/10/11	
5g	generalization	4/13/11	4/25/11	
6	child will have quiet hands for 1 minute	5/1/11	5/20/11	
6g	generalization	5/22/11	6/13/11	

Basic Programs

Child Name:. . . . .

Quiet Hands

Teaching Procedure: Present the child with the direction "QUIET HANDS OR HANDS DOWN."

Prompt Hierarchy: Use the least intrusive prompt required in order for the child to be successful (no prompt, gestural, faded physical, physical).

Materials: None.

Note: Quiet hands can either be by the child's side or in front of them placed on a table.

program started:		program mastered:		
	STEPS	STARTED	MASTERED	COMMENTS
1	child will have quiet hands for 3 seconds			
1g	generalization			
2	child will have quiet hands for 6 seconds			
2g	generalization			
3	child will have quiet hands for 10 seconds			
3g	generalization			
4	child will have quiet hands for 20 seconds			
4g	generalization			
5	child will have quiet hands for 30 seconds			
5g	generalization			
6	child will have quiet hands for 1 minute			
6g	generalization			

Child Name: . . . .

Attending

Teaching Procedure: Present the child with the direction "SIT QUIET." This means hands on lap/table, feet on floor, and the child is facing the instructor. The child does not need to meet eye to eye with the instructor just as long as the child is facing the instructor and the instructor knows the child is attending.

Prompt Hierarchy: Use the least intrusive prompt required in order for the child to be successful (no prompt, gesture, faded physical, physical).

Materials: None.

program started:		program mastered:		
	STEPS	STARTED	MASTERED	COMMENTS
1	child will attend within 10 seconds of the direction being presented			
1g	generalization			
2	child will attend within 5 seconds of the direction being presented			
2g	generalization			
3	child will attend within 3 seconds of the direction being presented			
3g	generalization			

Child Name:. . . . .

Responds to Name

Teaching Procedure: Present the child with the direction: PRESENT CHILD'S NAME. Follow the steps below.

Prompt Hierarchy: Use the least intrusive prompt required in order for the child to be successful (no prompt, gestural, faded physical, physical).

Materials: None.

program started:		program mastered:		
	STEPS	**STARTED**	**MASTERED**	**COMMENTS**
1	will respond to name being called within 5 seconds by looking at the person			
1g	generalization			
2	will respond to name being called within 3 seconds by looking at the person			
2g	generalization			
3	will respond to name being called within 1 second by looking at the person			
3g	generalization			

Child Name: . . . .

Eye Contact

Teaching Procedure: Present the child with the direction "LOOK AT ME."

Prompt Hierarchy: Use the least intrusive prompt required in order for the child to be successful (no prompt, gesture, faded physical, physical).

Materials: None.

Note: Although there is a direction provided, try to not use any direction. Try to get the child to naturally look at you without adding a verbal direction.

program started:		program mastered:		
	STEPS	STARTED	MASTERED	COMMENTS
1	maintains eye contact for first 3 seconds			
1g	generalization			
2	maintains eye contact for first 6 seconds			
2g	generalization			
3	maintains eye contact for first 10 seconds			
3g	generalization			

Child Name:..

Pointing Program

Teaching Procedure: Present the child with the direction "POINT TO [NAME OBJECT]" and follow the steps below.

Prompt Hierarchy: Use the least intrusive prompt required in order for the child to be successful (no prompt, gestural, faded physical, physical).

Materials: Objects/pictures that the child is familiar with.

program started:		program mastered:		
	STEPS	STARTED	MASTERED	COMMENTS
1	will point to item when presented immediately in front of the student within 3 seconds			
1g	generalization			
2	will point to item when presented in a down position within 3 seconds			
2g	generalization			
3	will point to item when presented on the right side position within 3 seconds			
3g	generalization			
4	will point to item when presented on the left side position within 3 seconds			
4g	generalization			

Child Name:. . . . .

Responds to Various Directions to Identify an Object/Picture/Item

Teaching Procedure: Present the child with the direction: STATE THE DIRECTION IN EACH STEP.

Prompt Hierarchy: Use the least intrusive prompt required in order for the child to be successful (no prompt, gesture faded physical, physical).

Materials: Objects/pictures/items that the child is familiar with.

program started:		program mastered:		
	STEPS	**STARTED**	**MASTERED**	**COMMENTS**
1	child will "point to" known object/picture/item			
1g	generalization			
2	child will "touch" known object/picture/item			
2g	generalization			
3	child will "give me" known object/picture/item			
3g	generalization			
4	child will "find" known object/picture/item			
4g	generalization			
5	child will "show me" known object/picture/item			
5g	generalization			
6	child will respond to "where is the" known object/picture/item			
6g	generalization			

Behavior Programs

Child Name: . . . .

Wait Program

Teaching Procedure: Get the child to mand for an item that they want. Then tell the child "you need to wait."

Prompt Hierarchy: Use the least intrusive prompt required in order for the child to be successful (no prompt, gesture, faded physical, physical).

Materials: Strong reinforcers.

Note: A mand is when the child communicates their wants and needs to another person *without* being asked "What do you want?" It can be in the form of a gesture, sign language, picture exchange, or words. The point of manding is to get the child to be able to walk up to another person and be able to "mand" for the item that they want. You can think of a mand as the child demanding or requesting an item.

program started:		program mastered:		
	STEPS	**STARTED**	**MASTERED**	**COMMENTS**
1	child will wait for 5 seconds before getting the requested item			
1g	generalization			
2	child will wait for 10 seconds before getting the requested item			
2g	generalization			
3	child will wait for 20 seconds before getting the requested item			
3g	generalization			
4	child will wait for 30 seconds before getting the requested item			
4g	generalization			

5	child will wait for 1 minute before getting the requested item			
5g	generalization			
6	child will wait for 3 minutes before getting the requested item			
6g	generalization			
7	child will wait for 5 minutes before getting the requested item			
7g	generalization			

Child Name: . . . .

Transition

Teaching Procedure: Present the child with the direction "TIME TO GO TO _____ [NAME ACTIVITY]."

Prompt Hierarchy: Use the least intrusive prompt required in order for the child to be successful (no prompt, gesture, faded physical, physical).

Materials: None.

program started:		program mastered:		
	STEPS	**STARTED**	**MASTERED**	**COMMENTS**
1	will transition from a non-preferred activity to a preferred activity			
1g	generalization			
2	will transition from a preferred activity to a preferred activity			
2g	generalization			
3	will transition from a preferred activity to a non-preferred activity			
3g	generalization			
4	will transition from a non-preferred activity to a non-preferred activity			
4g	generalization			

Child Name:. . . . .

Desensitization to Touch

Teaching Procedure: Present the child with the direction "GIVE ME A _____."

Prompt Hierarchy: Use the least intrusive prompt required in order for the child to be successful (no prompt, gesture, faded physical, physical).

Materials: None.

program started:		program mastered:		
	STEPS	STARTED	MASTERED	COMMENTS
1	high 5			
1g	generalization			
2	pat on the back			
2g	generalization			
3	hug			
3g	generalization			
4	hold hands			
4g	generalization			

Child Name: . . . .

Desensitization to Dentist

Teaching Procedure: This program will be taught in the home for the first 3 steps, then the program will switch to actually being at the dentist office. Each step will walk you through what should be done and how.

Prompt Hierarchy: Use the least intrusive prompt required in order for the child to be successful (no prompt, gesture, faded physical, physical).

Materials: There are children's books about going to the dentist. It is recommended that you read some of these books to your child while teaching working on this program. You will also need a toothbrush and a mirror that will fit in their mouth, then an actual dental office and dentist.

Note: When teaching this program, use a highly reinforcing item, and as soon as they complete the task in each step, they get their reinforcer. Example: in step 4, they go to the dentist office and sit in the chair. The dentist comes in and says hi; as soon as the dentist leaves say "great job at the dentist, here is your ___ (reinforcer)."

program started:		program mastered:		
	STEPS	**STARTED**	**MASTERED**	**COMMENTS**
1	*Let's pretend we are going to the dentist. You (the child) be the dentist first;* let the child just do what they want. You can suggest things for them to do.			
1g	generalization			
2	*Let's pretend we are going to the dentist. It is my (teacher/parent) turn to be the dentist. You (child) sit in the chair and say "ah" or open mouth.*			
2g	generalization			

3	*Let's pretend we are going to the dentist. It is my (teacher/parent) turn to be the dentist. You (child) sit in the chair and say "ah" or open mouth*; then take a toothbrush and put it in their mouth for a couple of seconds. If you can, brush their teeth for a couple of seconds.			
3g	generalization			
4	*It's time to go to the dentist.* This time you will actually go to the dentist office and have the child sit in the dental chair for a couple of seconds. Then end the appointment. The dentist should not actually work on the child. They should be in the room when the child is sitting in the chair though.			
4g	generalization			
5	*It's time to go to the dentist.* Have the child sit in the dental chair and have the dentist just look in their mouth today.			
5g	generalization			
6	*It's time to go to the dentist.* Have the child sit in the dental chair and have the dentist perform the work.			
6g	generalization			

Child Name: . . . .

Desensitization to Doctor

Teaching Procedure: This program will be taught in the home for the first 2 steps, then the program will switch to actually being at the doctor's. Each step will walk you through what should be done and how.

Prompt Hierarchy: Use the least intrusive prompt required in order for the child to be successful (no prompt, gesture, faded physical, physical).

Materials: Kids' doctor's kit, real doctor and doctor office.

Note: When teaching this program, use a highly reinforcing item, and as soon as they complete the task in each step, they get their reinforcer. Example: in step 3, they go to the doctor's office and sit in the exam room. The doctor comes in and says hi; as soon as the doctor leaves say "great job at the doctor, here is your ___ (reinforcer)."

program started:		program mastered:		
	STEPS	**STARTED**	**MASTERED**	**COMMENTS**
1	*Let's pretend we are going to the doctor. You (the child) be the doctor first;* let the child just do what they want. You can suggest things for them to do. Make sure you give them the kids' doctor's kit to play with.			
1g	generalization			
2	*Let's pretend we are going to the doctor. It is my (teacher/parent) turn to be the doctor.* Use the kids' doctor's kit and look in the child's ear and throat. Also listen to their chest.			
2g	generalization			
3	*It's time to go to the doctor.* This time you will actually go to the doctor office and have the child sit in the exam room. Have the doctor come in and just say hi. Then end the appointment.			
3g	generalization			
4	*It's time to go to the doctor.* This time the doctor will examine the child.			
4g	generalization			

Child Name:. . . . .

Desensitization to Haircuts

Teaching Procedure: Present the child with the direction "IT'S TIME FOR A HAIRCUT" and follow the steps below.

Prompt Hierarchy: Use the least intrusive prompt required in order for the child to be successful (no prompt, gesture, faded physical, physical).

Materials: Play-doh scissors, smock, hair dresser, hair dresser shop.

Note: Generalization should include other people giving the haircut (until you actually get to the hair dresser, then it should be a consistent hair dresser).

program started:		program mastered:		
	STEPS	**STARTED**	**MASTERED**	**COMMENTS**
1	Tell the child: *Let's pretend to get a haircut. You (child) be the hair dresser first.* Tell the child to put a smock on you and then let the child just do what they want.			
1g	generalization			
2	*It's time for a haircut, sit down in the chair. I am going to put a smock on you.* Then just take your hand and start to touch the child's hair. End the haircut here.			
2g	generalization			
3	*It's time for a haircut, sit down in the chair. I am going to put a smock on you.* Then just take your hand and start to touch the child's hair. Then take the play-doh scissors and pretend to cut the child's hair.			
3g	generalization			

4	*It's time for a haircut, let's get in the car.* This time have the child go into the hair dresser and sit in the hair dresser's chair. Let the hair dresser just touch the child's hair and end the haircut at this point. When the child is sitting in the chair, give them something to play with or eat to help distract them. Make sure the toy/food is very reinforcing.			
4g	generalization			
5	*It's time for a haircut, let's get in the car.* This time have the child go into the hair dresser and sit in the hair dresser's chair. Let the hair dresser just touch the child's hair first, then they can start actually cutting the hair. When the child is sitting in the chair, give them something to play with or eat to help distract them. Make sure the toy/food is very reinforcing.			
5g	generalization			

Child Name: . . . .

Clean Up

Teaching Procedure: Have the child play with toys. When finished playing, present the child with the direction "CLEAN UP."

Prompt Hierarchy: Use the least intrusive prompt required in order for the child to be successful (no prompt, gestural, faded physical, physical).

Materials: Toys.

Note: This program is taught using backward chaining. The program can either be taught using 1 toy with many pieces (like a puzzle or Lego) or using more than 1 toy with single pieces (book).

program started:		program mastered:		
	STEPS	**STARTED**	**MASTERED**	**COMMENTS**
1	child will pick up the last piece of 1 toy/the last toy			
1g	generalization			
2	child will pick up the last 2 pieces of 1 toy/or the last 2 toys			
2g	generalization			
3	child will pick up the last 3 pieces of 1 toy/or the last 3 toys			
3g	generalization			
4	child will pick up the last 4 pieces of 1 toy/or the remaining 4 toys			
4g	generalization			

Motor Programs

Child Name:. . . . .

Gross Motor Imitation

Teaching Procedure: Present the child with the direction "DO THIS ___."

Prompt Hierarchy: Use the least intrusive prompt required in order for the child to be successful (no prompt, gestural, faded physical, physical).

Materials: None.

program started:		program mastered:		
	STEPS	STARTED	MASTERED	COMMENTS
1	clap hands			
1g	generalization			
2	arms up			
2g	generalization			
3	stamp feet			
3g	generalization			
4	tap table			
4g	generalization			
5	arms to side			
5g	generalization			
6	pat tummy			
6g	generalization			
7	rub hands together			
7g	generalization			
8	hand on head			
8g	generalization			
9	arms out in front			
9g	generalization			
10	touch toes			
10g	generalization			

11	stomp 1 foot			
11g	generalization			
12	cross legs sitting			
12g	generalization			
13	lift and hold 1 leg			
13g	generalization			
14	place feet together			
14g	generalization			
15	spread feet apart			
15g	generalization			
16	hop			
16g	generalization			
17	lift foot and shake			
17g	generalization			
18	cross legs standing			
18g	generalization			
19	place foot forward			
19g	generalization			
20	bend side to side at waist			
20g	generalization			
21	shake head yes			
21g	generalization			
22	shake head no			
22g	generalization			
23	move head side to side			
23g	generalization			

Child Name:. . . . .

Motor Imitation

Teaching Procedure: Present the child with the direction "DO THIS ___."

Prompt Hierarchy: Use the least intrusive prompt required in order for the child to be successful (no prompt, gestural, faded physical, physical).

Materials: Car, cup, spoon, hammer, doll, drums, bowl, hat.

program started:		program mastered:		
	STEPS	STARTED	MASTERED	COMMENTS
1	roll car back and forth			
1g	generalization			
2	drink from a cup			
2g	generalization			
3	stir a spoon in cup			
3g	generalization			
4	bang a hammer			
4g	generalization			
5	feed doll			
5g	generalization			
6	brush hair			
6g	generalization			
7	play drums			
7g	generalization			
8	kiss a doll			
8g	generalization			
9	put object in bowl			
9g	generalization			
10	put hat on			
10g	generalization			

Child Name: . . . .

Fine Motor Imitation

Teaching Procedure: Present the child with the direction "DO THIS ___."

Prompt Hierarchy: Use the least intrusive prompt required in order for the child to be successful (no prompt, gestural, faded physical, physical).

Materials: None.

program started:		program mastered:		
	STEPS	STARTED	MASTERED	COMMENTS
1	touch thumbs together and hold			
1g	generalization			
2	touch thumb and pointer finger together			
2g	generalization			
3	bounce thumb and pointer finger			
3g	generalization			
4	spread fingers apart			
4g	generalization			
5	touch pointer fingers together			
5g	generalization			
6	touch middle fingers together			
6g	generalization			
7	touch ring fingers together			
7g	generalization			
8	touch pinky fingers together			
8g	generalization			
9	bend fingers down			
9g	generalization			
10	touch thumb and middle finger together			
10g	generalization			

Child Name:. . . . .

Oral Motor Imitation

Teaching Procedure: Present the child with the direction "DO THIS ___."

Prompt Hierarchy: Use the least intrusive prompt required in order for the child to be successful (no prompt, gestural, faded physical, physical).

Materials: None.

program started:		program mastered:		
	STEPS	**STARTED**	**MASTERED**	**COMMENTS**
1	open mouth			
1g	generalization			
2	open and close mouth			
2g	generalization			
3	blow (like you are blowing bubbles)			
3g	generalization			
4	lips together and blow (making raspberries with your mouth)			
4g	generalization			
5	stick your tongue out			
5g	generalization			
6	stick your tongue in and out			
6g	generalization			

Child Name: . . . .

Color Between the Lines

Teaching Procedure: Present the child with the direction "COLOR."

Prompt Hierarchy: Use the least intrusive prompt required in order for the child to be successful (no prompt, gesture, faded physical, physical).

Materials: Crayons, paper.

program started:		program mastered:		
	STEPS	**STARTED**	**MASTERED**	**COMMENTS**
1	can color a large shape staying within the boundaries approximately 4 square inches or less			
1g	generalization			
2	can color a large shape staying within the boundaries approximately 2 square inches or less			
2g	generalization			

Child Name: . . . .

Copy Straight Lines

Teaching Procedure: Present the child with the direction "DO THIS."

Prompt Hierarchy: Use the least intrusive prompt required in order for the child to be successful (no prompt, gesture, faded physical, physical).

Materials: Pencil or crayons, paper.

program started:		program mastered:		
	STEPS	STARTED	MASTERED	COMMENTS
1	can copy a straight line that is up and down			
1g	generalization			
2	can copy a straight line that is horizontal			
2g	generalization			
3	can copy a diagonal line			
3g	generalization			
4	can copy a square			
4g	generalization			
5	can copy a rectangle			
5g	generalization			
6	can copy a triangle			
6g	generalization			

Receptive Programs

Child Name: . . . .

One Step Directions

Teaching Procedure: Present the child with the direction: STATE THE DIRECTION (E.G. CLAP HANDS). Follow the steps below.

Prompt Hierarchy: Use the least intrusive prompt required in order for the child to be successful (no prompt, gestural, faded physical, physical).

Materials: None.

program started:		program mastered:		
	STEPS	STARTED	MASTERED	COMMENTS
1	clap hands			
1g	generalization			
2	stand up			
2g	generalization			
3	sit down			
3g	generalization			
4	jump			
4g	generalization			
5	wave			
5g	generalization			
6	turn around			
6g	generalization			
7	blow			
7g	generalization			
8	come here			
8g	generalization			
9	stomp feet			
9g	generalization			
10	knock			
10g	generalization			

Child Name: . . . .

Two Step Directions

Teaching Procedure: Present the child with the direction: VERBALLY STATE THE DIRECTIONS [E.G. STAND UP, GET TOY].

Prompt Hierarchy: Use the least intrusive prompt required in order for the child to be successful (no prompt, gestural, faded physical, physical).

Materials: Toy, paper, tissue, garbage, puzzle.

program started:		program mastered:		
	STEPS	STARTED	MASTERED	COMMENTS
1	stand up, get toy			
1g	generalization			
2	stand up, turn around			
2g	generalization			
3	get paper, sit down			
3g	generalization			
4	get tissue, wipe your nose			
4g	generalization			
5	wipe your nose, throw out tissue			
5g	generalization			

Child Name: . . . .

Receptive Identification of Pictures

Teaching Procedure: Present the child with the direction "TOUCH/POINT TO/SHOW ME ___ [NAME PICTURE]."

Prompt Hierarchy: Use the least intrusive prompt required in order for the child to be successful (no prompt, gesture, faded physical, physical).

Materials: Pictures presented in the steps below.

Note: Generalization should include pointing to pictures in books or magazines.

program started:		program mastered:		
	STEPS	**STARTED**	**MASTERED**	**COMMENTS**
1	table			
1g	generalization			
2	chair			
2g	generalization			
3	door			
3g	generalization			
4	sink			
4g	generalization			
5	toilet			
5g	generalization			
6	spoon			
6g	generalization			
7	plate			
7g	generalization			
8	book			
8g	generalization			
9	toy			

9g	generalization			
10	crayon			
10g	generalization			
11	paper			
11g	generalization			
12	computer			
12g	generalization			
13	window			
13g	generalization			
14	teddy bear			
14g	generalization			
15	candy			
15g	generalization			
16	camera			
16g	generalization			
17	phone			
17g	generalization			
18	sock			
18g	generalization			
19	shoe			
19g	generalization			

Child Name: . . . .

Receptive Identification of Objects

Teaching Procedure: Present the child with the direction "TOUCH/POINT TO/SHOW ME ___ [NAME OBJECT]."

Prompt Hierarchy: Use the least intrusive prompt required in order for the child to be successful (no prompt, gesture, faded physical, physical).

Materials: Objects presented in the steps below.

program started:		program mastered:		
	STEPS	STARTED	MASTERED	COMMENTS
1	sock			
1g	generalization			
2	shoe			
2g	generalization			
3	pencil			
3g	generalization			
4	paper			
4g	generalization			
5	crayon			
5g	generalization			
6	cup			
6g	generalization			
7	camera			
7g	generalization			
8	phone			
8g	generalization			

9	television			
9g	generalization			
10	door			
10g	generalization			
11	toilet			
11g	generalization			
12	sink			
12g	generalization			
13	book			
13g	generalization			
14	balloons			
14g	generalization			
15	table			
15g	generalization			
16	chair			
16g	generalization			
17	teddy bear			
17g	generalization			
18	candy			
18g	generalization			
19	blocks			
19g	generalization			

Child Name:. . . . .

Receptive Identification of Body Parts

Teaching Procedure: Present the child with the direction "TOUCH [BODY PART]."

Prompt Hierarchy: Use the least intrusive prompt required in order for the child to be successful (no prompt, gestural, faded physical, physical).

Materials: Dolls, pictures.

Note: Generalization of this program should be touching body parts on other items: other people, dolls, pictures, etc.

program started:		program mastered:		
	STEPS	STARTED	MASTERED	COMMENTS
1	nose			
1g	generalization			
2	eyes			
2g	generalization			
3	ears			
3g	generalization			
4	mouth			
4g	generalization			
5	arm			
5g	generalization			
6	leg			
6g	generalization			
7	foot			
7g	generalization			
8	hand			

8g	generalization			
9	elbow			
9g	generalization			
10	knee			
10g	generalization			
11	chin			
11g	generalization			
12	head			
12g	generalization			
13	hair			
13g	generalization			
14	back			
14g	generalization			
15	stomach			
15g	generalization			
16	forehead			
16g	generalization			
17	neck			
17g	generalization			
18	tongue			
18g	generalization			

Child Name:. . . . .

Receptive Identification of Articles of Clothing

Teaching Procedure: In a field of 3 or more, lay out the articles of clothing and ask the child to "TOUCH/POINT/SHOW ME ____ [NAME ARTICLE OF CLOTHING]."

Prompt Hierarchy: Use the least intrusive prompt required in order for the child to be successful (no prompt, gesture faded physical, physical).

Materials: Various articles of clothing including pictures of clothing and actual articles of clothing.

Note: Generalization should include identifying articles of clothing on self and other people, in books, and on dolls.

program started:		program mastered:		
	STEPS	**STARTED**	**MASTERED**	**COMMENTS**
1	shirt			
1g	generalization			
2	pants			
2g	generalization			
3	socks			
3g	generalization			
4	shoes			
4g	generalization			
5	underwear/diaper			
5g	generalization			
6	shorts			
6g	generalization			
7	jacket			
7g	generalization			
8	hat			
8g	generalization			
9	gloves			
9g	generalization			

Child Name: . . . .

Receptive Identification of Familiar People

Teaching Procedure: Present the child with the direction "TOUCH/POINT TO/SHOW ME ___ [NAME THE PERSON]."

Prompt Hierarchy: Use the least intrusive prompt required in order for the child to be successful (no prompt, gesture, faded physical, physical).

Materials: Pictures of people stated below.

Note: Generalization should be actual person and other pictures of the person, in addition to the child being presented with the picture in different settings and with different people.

program started:		program mastered:		
	STEPS	**STARTED**	**MASTERED**	**COMMENTS**
1	mom			
1g	generalization			
2	dad			
2g	generalization			
3	sibling			
3g	generalization			
4	grandmother			
4g	generalization			
5	teacher			
5g	generalization			
6	friend			
6g	generalization			

Child Name: . . . .

Receptive Identification of Emotions

Teaching Procedure: Present the child with the direction "TOUCH ___ [NAME THE EMOTION]."

Prompt Hierarchy: Use the least intrusive prompt required in order for the child to be successful (no prompt, gestural, faded physical, physical).

Materials: Picture cards of the emotions. You can obtain picture cards of emotions through the websites www.do2learn.com and www.difflearn.com. You can also take pictures of yourself demonstrating different emotions.

Note: Generalization should include identifying emotions through pictures, television, books, magazines, and on people.

program started:		program mastered:		
	STEPS	**STARTED**	**MASTERED**	**COMMENTS**
1	happy			
1g	generalization			
2	sad			
2g	generalization			
3	angry/mad			
3g	generalization			
4	surprised			
4g	generalization			
5	scared			
5g	generalization			
6	bored			
6g	generalization			
7	embarrassed			
7g	generalization			

Child Name: . . . .

Receptive Identification of Community Helpers

Teaching Procedure: Present the child with the direction "SHOW ME/POINT TO/TOUCH ____ [COMMUNITY HELPER]."

Prompt Hierarchy: Use the least intrusive prompt required in order for the child to be successful (no prompt, gestural, faded physical, physical).

Materials: Pictures of items below.

program started:		program mastered:		
	STEPS	**STARTED**	**MASTERED**	**COMMENTS**
1	policeman			
1g	generalization			
2	fireman			
2g	generalization			
3	mail man			
3g	generalization			
4	doctor			
4g	generalization			
5	nurse			
5g	generalization			
6	bus driver			
6g	generalization			
7	waiter			
7g	generalization			
8	teacher			
8g	generalization			

Child Name:. . . . .

Receptive Identification of Environmental Sounds

Teaching Procedure: Present the child with the direction "WHAT SOUND DO YOU HEAR?" [CHILD WILL POINT/TOUCH THE CORRECT SOUND].

Prompt Hierarchy: Use the least intrusive prompt required in order for the child to be successful (no prompt, gestural, faded physical, physical).

Materials: Sounds of steps below, pictures of steps below.

program started:		program mastered:		
	STEPS	**STARTED**	**MASTERED**	**COMMENTS**
1	dog			
1g	generalization			
2	fire truck			
2g	generalization			
3	train			
3g	generalization			
4	horn (on car)			
4g	generalization			
5	airplane			
5g	generalization			
6	ambulance			
6g	generalization			
7	bird			
7g	generalization			
8	telephone ringing			
8g	generalization			
9	door bell			
9g	generalization			
10	baby crying			
10g	generalization			

Expressive Programs

Child Name: . . . .

Expressive Identification of Pictures

Teaching Procedure: Present the child with the direction "WHAT IS THIS? _____ [WHILE HOLDING UP PICTURE/POINTING TO PICTURE]."

Prompt Hierarchy: Use the least intrusive prompt required in order for the child to be successful (no prompt, faded verbal, verbal).

Materials: Objects presented in the steps below.

program started:		program mastered:		
	STEPS	**STARTED**	**MASTERED**	**COMMENTS**
1	table			
1g	generalization			
2	chair			
2g	generalization			
3	door			
3g	generalization			
4	sink			
4g	generalization			
5	toilet			
5g	generalization			
6	spoon			
6g	generalization			
7	plate			
7g	generalization			
8	book			
8g	generalization			

9	toy			
9g	generalization			
10	crayon			
10g	generalization			
11	paper			
11g	generalization			
12	computer			
12g	generalization			
13	window			
13g	generalization			
14	teddy bear			
14g	generalization			
15	candy			
15g	generalization			
16	camera			
16g	generalization			
17	phone			
17g	generalization			
18	sock			
18g	generalization			
19	shoe			
19g	generalization			

Child Name: . . . .

Expressive Identification of Objects

Teaching Procedure: Present the child with the direction "WHAT IS THIS? _____ [WHILE HOLDING UP OBJECT/POINTING TO OBJECT]."

Prompt Hierarchy: Use the least intrusive prompt required in order for the child to be successful (no prompt, faded verbal, verbal).

Materials: Objects presented in the steps below.

program started:		program mastered:		
	STEPS	**STARTED**	**MASTERED**	**COMMENTS**
1	sock			
1g	generalization			
2	shoe			
2g	generalization			
3	pencil			
3g	generalization			
4	paper			
4g	generalization			
5	crayon			
5g	generalization			
6	cup			
6g	generalization			
7	camera			
7g	generalization			
8	phone			
8g	generalization			

9	television			
9g	generalization			
10	door			
10g	generalization			
11	toilet			
11g	generalization			
12	sink			
12g	generalization			
13	book			
13g	generalization			
14	balloons			
14g	generalization			
15	table			
15g	generalization			
16	chair			
16g	generalization			
17	teddy bear			
17g	generalization			
18	candy			
18g	generalization			
19	blocks			
19g	generalization			

Child Name: . . . .

Expressive Identification of Body Parts

Teaching Procedure: Present the child with the direction POINT TO A BODY PART AND ASK CHILD TO NAME IT.

Prompt Hierarchy: Use the least intrusive prompt required in order for the child to be successful (no prompt, faded verbal, verbal).

Materials: Dolls, pictures.

Note: Generalization of this program should be labeling body parts on other items: other people, dolls, pictures, etc.

program started:		program mastered:		
	STEPS	**STARTED**	**MASTERED**	**COMMENTS**
1	nose			
1g	generalization			
2	eyes			
2g	generalization			
3	ears			
3g	generalization			
4	mouth			
4g	generalization			
5	arm			
5g	generalization			
6	leg			
6g	generalization			
7	foot			
7g	generalization			
8	hand			

8g	generalization			
9	elbow			
9g	generalization			
10	knee			
10g	generalization			
11	chin			
11g	generalization			
12	head			
12g	generalization			
13	hair			
13g	generalization			
14	back			
14g	generalization			
15	stomach			
15g	generalization			
16	forehead			
16g	generalization			
17	neck			
17g	generalization			
18	tongue			
18g	generalization			

Child Name: . . . .

Expressive Identification of Articles of Clothing

Teaching Procedure: Hold up the article of clothing and ask the child "WHAT IS IT?" Generalization should include identifying the clothing on self and on others.

Prompt Hierarchy: Use the least intrusive prompt required in order for the child to be successful (no prompt, faded verbal, verbal).

Materials: Various articles of clothing.

program started:		program mastered:		
	STEPS	**STARTED**	**MASTERED**	**COMMENTS**
1	shirt			
1g	generalization			
2	pants			
2g	generalization			
3	socks			
3g	generalization			
4	shoes			
4g	generalization			
5	underwear/diaper			
5g	generalization			
6	shorts			
6g	generalization			
7	jacket			
7g	generalization			
8	hat			
8g	generalization			
9	gloves			
9g	generalization			

Child Name: ....

Expressive Identification of Familiar People

Teaching Procedure: Present the child with the direction "WHO IS THIS? _____ [WHILE HOLDING UP PICTURE]."

Prompt Hierarchy: Use the least intrusive prompt required in order for the child to be successful (no prompt, faded verbal, verbal).

Materials: Pictures of people stated below.

Note: Generalization should be actual person and other pictures of the person, in addition to the child being presented with the picture in different settings and with different people.

program started:		program mastered:		
	STEPS	**STARTED**	**MASTERED**	**COMMENTS**
1	mom			
1g	generalization			
2	dad			
2g	generalization			
3	sibling			
3g	generalization			
4	grandmother			
4g	generalization			
5	teacher			
5g	generalization			
6	friend			
6g	generalization			

Child Name: . . . .

Expressive Identification of Emotions

Teaching Procedure: Direction: "HOW IS THE PERSON FEELING?"

Prompt Hierarchy: Use the least intrusive prompt required in order for the child to be successful (no prompt, faded verbal, verbal).

Materials: Picture cards of the emotions. You can obtain picture cards of emotions through the websites www.do2learn.com and www.difflearn.com. You can also take pictures of yourself demonstrating different emotions.

Note: Generalization should be actual people acting out the emotion which can include television.

program started:		program mastered:		
	STEPS	**STARTED**	**MASTERED**	**COMMENTS**
1	happy			
1g	generalization			
2	sad			
2g	generalization			
3	angry/mad			
3g	generalization			
4	surprised			
4g	generalization			
5	scared			
5g	generalization			
6	bored			
6g	generalization			
7	embarrassed			
7g	generalization			

Child Name: . . . .

Expressive Identification of Community Helpers

Teaching Procedure: Present the child with the direction "WHO IS THIS PERSON? _____ [WHILE HOLDING UP PICTURE/POINTING TO PICTURE]."

Prompt Hierarchy: Use the least intrusive prompt required in order for the child to be successful (no prompt, faded verbal, verbal).

Materials: Pictures presented in the steps below.

Note: Generalization should try to include the child identifying an actual community helper, and not just through pictures.

program started:		program mastered:		
	STEPS	**STARTED**	**MASTERED**	**COMMENTS**
1	policeman			
1g	generalization			
2	fireman			
2g	generalization			
3	mail man			
3g	generalization			
4	doctor			
4g	generalization			
5	nurse			
5g	generalization			
6	bus driver			
6g	generalization			
7	waiter			
7g	generalization			
8	teacher			
8g	generalization			

Child Name: . . . .

Expressive Identification of Environmental Sounds

Teaching Procedure: Present the child with the direction "WHAT SOUND DO YOU HEAR?"

Prompt Hierarchy: Use the least intrusive prompt required in order for the child to be successful (no prompt, faded verbal, verbal).

Materials: Sounds of a dog barking, a fire truck siren, a train whistle, a horn, an airplane, an ambulance siren, a bird chirping, a telephone ringing, a door bell, a baby crying.

program started:		program mastered:		
	STEPS	**STARTED**	**MASTERED**	**COMMENTS**
1	dog			
1g	generalization			
2	fire truck			
2g	generalization			
3	train			
3g	generalization			
4	horn (on car)			
4g	generalization			
5	airplane			
5g	generalization			
6	ambulance			
6g	generalization			
7	bird			
7g	generalization			
8	telephone ringing			
8g	generalization			
9	door bell			
9g	generalization			
10	baby crying			
10g	generalization			

Action Programs

Child Name: . . . .

Receptive Identification of Actions

Teaching Procedure: Present the child with the direction: "SHOW ME/POINT TO/TOUCH _____ [ACTION]."

Prompt Hierarchy: Use the least intrusive prompt required in order for the child to be successful (no prompt, gestural, faded physical, physical).

Materials: Pictures of items below.

program started:		program mastered:		
	STEPS	STARTED	MASTERED	COMMENTS
1	jumping			
1g	generalization			
2	hopping			
2g	generalization			
3	walking			
3g	generalization			
4	sleeping			
4g	generalization			
5	hugging			
5g	generalization			
6	sitting			
6g	generalization			
7	drinking			
7g	generalization			
8	eating			
8g	generalization			

9	falling			
9g	generalization			
10	playing			
10g	generalization			
11	cutting			
11g	generalization			
12	crying			
12g	generalization			
13	brushing			
13g	generalization			
14	blowing			
14g	generalization			
15	dancing			
15g	generalization			
16	crawling			
16g	generalization			
17	reading			
17g	generalization			
18	drawing			
18g	generalization			

Child Name:. . . . .

Expressive Identification of Actions

Teaching Procedure: Present the child with the direction "WHAT IS THE PERSON DOING? _____ [WHILE HOLDING UP PICTURE/POINTING TO PICTURE]."

Prompt Hierarchy: Use the least intrusive prompt required in order for the child to be successful (no prompt, faded verbal, verbal).

Materials: Pictures presented in the steps below.

Note: Generalization should include an actual person acting out the action with the direction "What am I doing?"

program started:		program mastered:		
	STEPS	**STARTED**	**MASTERED**	**COMMENTS**
1	jumping			
1g	generalization			
2	hopping			
2g	generalization			
3	walking			
3g	generalization			
4	sleeping			
4g	generalization			
5	hugging			
5g	generalization			
6	sitting			
6g	generalization			
7	drinking			
7g	generalization			
8	eating			

8g	generalization			
9	falling			
9g	generalization			
10	playing			
10g	generalization			
11	cutting			
11g	generalization			
12	crying			
12g	generalization			
13	brushing			
13g	generalization			
14	blowing			
14g	generalization			
15	dancing			
15g	generalization			
16	crawling			
16g	generalization			
17	reading			
17g	generalization			
18	drawing			
18g	generalization			

Child Name: . . . .

Imitates Actions of Others

Teaching Procedure: Start to do the action while making sure the child is attending. Do not ask the child to do what you are doing, or to look at you. The purpose of this program is for the child to start to naturally pick up on what you/others are doing and just imitate them.

Prompt Hierarchy: Use the least intrusive prompt required in order for the child to be successful (no prompt, gesture, faded physical, physical).

Materials: None.

program started:		program mastered:		
	STEPS	**STARTED**	**MASTERED**	**COMMENTS**
1	clap hands			
1g	generalization			
2	stamp feet			
2g	generalization			
3	jump			
3g	generalization			
4	sit down			
4g	generalization			
5	stand up			
5g	generalization			

Child Name: . . . .

Imitates Two Step Action

Teaching Procedure: Present the child with the direction "DO THIS _____".

Prompt Hierarchy: Use the least intrusive prompt required in order for the child to be successful (no prompt, gesture, faded physical, physical).

Materials: None.

program started:		program mastered:		
	STEPS	**STARTED**	**MASTERED**	**COMMENTS**
1	clap hands, tap thighs (after model has finished)			
1g	generalization			
2	stand up, turn around (after model has finished)			
2g	generalization			
3	tap table, wave (after model has finished)			
3g	generalization			
4	arms up, arms on hips (after model has finished)			
4g	generalization			
5	touch head, hands on shoulders (after model has finished)			
5g	generalization			
6	stamp feet, clap hands (after model has finished)			
6g	generalization			
7	feet together, feet apart (after model has finished)			

7g	generalizationrub tummy, open mouth (after model has finished)			
8	rub tummy, open mouth (after model has finished)			
8g	generalization			
9	open and close mouth, wave (after model has finished)			
9g	generalization			
10	jump, sit down (after model has finished)			
10g	generalization			

Child Name: . . . .

Pretends to do an Action

Teaching Procedure: Present the child with the direction "SHOW ME HOW YOU _____ [NAME ACTION]."

Prompt Hierarchy: Use the least intrusive prompt required in order for the child to be successful (no prompt, gestural, faded physical, physical).

Materials: Dolls, pictures, actual articles of clothing.

Note: This program differs from expressive action identification in that the child is the one acting out the actions.

program started:		program mastered:		
	STEPS	STARTED	MASTERED	COMMENTS
1	laughing			
1g	generalization			
2	crying			
2g	generalization			
3	sleeping			
3g	generalization			
4	writing			
4g	generalization			
5	cutting			
5g	generalization			
6	jumping			
6g	generalization			
7	dancing			
7g	generalization			
8	reading			
8g	generalization			
9	eating			
9g	generalization			
10	drinking			
10g	generalization			

Communication Programs

Child Name: . . . .

Points to Communicate

Teaching Procedure: Present the child with the direction "SHOW ME WHAT YOU WANT."

Prompt Hierarchy: Use the least intrusive prompt required in order for the child to be successful (no prompt, gesture, faded physical, physical).

Materials: Preferred objects that the child would want.

program started:		program mastered:		
	STEPS	STARTED	MASTERED	COMMENTS
1	hold up reinforcing object and present direction			
1g	generalization			
2	hold up 2 reinforcing objects and present direction			
2g	generalization			
3	child will point to desired object in a field of 3 when presented with direction			
3g	generalization			
4	child will point to any known item when asked to find it			
4g	generalization			
5	child will show you what they want by pointing to it			
5g	generalization			

Child Name: . . . .

Yes/No

Teaching Procedure: Present the child with the direction "DO YOU WANT THIS ___?"

Prompt Hierarchy: Use the least intrusive prompt required in order for the child to be successful (non-verbal response = no prompt, gesture, faded physical, physical; verbal response = no prompt, faded verbal, verbal).

Materials: Preferred and non-preferred items.

Note: To identify a preferred item, allow the child to get up and play with what he or she wants. After 2–3 seconds of play, take item away and present the direction "Do you want this?" To make sure there is no confusion for non-preferred items, use something that is not a toy or a potential reinforcer.

program started:		program mastered:		
	STEPS	**STARTED**	**MASTERED**	**COMMENTS**
1	present the child with a preferred item and present direction			
1g	generalization			
2	present the child with a non-preferred item and present direction			
2g	generalization			
3	randomly present preferred and non-preferred items			
3g	generalization			

Child Name: . . . .

Manding

Teaching Procedure: Present the child with situations in which they would need to mand for the item/object/etc. (see steps below). If you provide them with the visual it is considered a prompted mand.

Prompt Hierarchy: Use the least intrusive prompt required in order for the child to be successful (no prompt, faded verbal, verbal).

Materials: None.

Note: A mand is when the child communicates their wants and needs to another person *without* being asked "What do you want?" It can be in the form of a gesture, sign language, picture exchange, or words. The point of manding is to get the child to be able to walk up to another person and be able to "mand" for the item that they want. You can think of a mand as the child demanding or requesting an item.

program started:		program mastered:		
	STEPS	**STARTED**	**MASTERED**	**COMMENTS**
1	open			
1g	generalization			
2	eat			
2g	generalization			
3	drink			
3g	generalization			
4	help me			
4g	generalization			
5	sit down			
5g	generalization			
6	stand up			
6g	generalization			
7	play			
7g	generalization			
8	close			
8g	generalization			
9	all done			
9g	generalization			

Child Name:. . . . .

Requests with Eye Contact

Teaching Procedure: Wait for the child to look at you before responding to their request. If the child does not look at you within 5 seconds of the request, prompt them.

Prompt Hierarchy: Use the least intrusive prompt required in order for the child to be successful (no prompt, gestural, faded physical, physical).

Materials: None.

Note: A request can be in the form of a gesture, sign language, picture exchange, or words.

program started:		program mastered:		
	STEPS	STARTED	MASTERED	COMMENTS
1	looks at person for a couple of seconds at some point during the request			
1g	generalization			
2	looks at person at the start of the request			
2g	generalization			
3	looks at person at the start of the request and at the end of the request			
3g	generalization			
4	looks at person for the entire request			
4g	generalization			

Child Name: . . . .

Gets Attention of Others

Teaching Procedure: Contrive a situation in which 1 person is busy. Tell the child to "GIVE ___ [THE BUSY PERSON] THE PIECE OF PAPER." Have the child walk over to the busy person and get their attention by either tapping their shoulder or calling their name.

Prompt Hierarchy: Use the least intrusive prompt required in order for the child to be successful (no prompt, gesture, faded physical, physical—for the tap; no prompt, faded verbal, verbal—to gain a person's attention by using their name).

Materials: None.

Note: Generalization should include using other directions than "give the paper to ___."

program started:		program mastered:		
	STEPS	**STARTED**	**MASTERED**	**COMMENTS**
1	will tap a person's shoulder to gain attention			
1g	generalization			
2	will call a person's name to gain attention			
2g	generalization			

Child Name: ....

Says Bye

Teaching Procedure: direction: A PERSON LEAVING.

Prompt Hierarchy: Use the least intrusive prompt required in order for the child to be successful (for a non-verbal child prompt a wave bye—no prompt, gesture, faded physical, physical; for a verbal child prompt the word bye—no prompt, faded verbal, verbal.

Materials: None.

program started:		program mastered:		
	STEPS	STARTED	MASTERED	COMMENTS
1	returns greeting			
1g	generalization			
2	initiates the goodbye when a person says "I am leaving"			
2g	generalization			

Child Name: ....

Says Hi

Teaching Procedure: Direction: THE ARRIVAL OF A PERSON.

Prompt Hierarchy: Use the least intrusive prompt required in order for the child to be successful (for a non-verbal child prompt a wave hello—no prompt, gesture, faded physical, physical; for a verbal child prompt the word hi—no prompt, faded verbal, verbal).

Materials: None.

program started:		program mastered:		
	STEPS	STARTED	MASTERED	COMMENTS
1	says "Hi" to person first			
1g	generalization			
2	responds with "Hi" when the person says "Hi" first			
2g	generalization			

Child Name:. . . . .

Imitates Sounds

Teaching Procedure: Present the child with the direction "SAY _____."

Prompt Hierarchy: Use the least intrusive prompt required in order for the child to be successful (no prompt, faded verbal, verbal).

Materials: None.

program started:		program mastered:		
	STEPS	**STARTED**	**MASTERED**	**COMMENTS**
1	/a/			
1g	generalization			
2	/m/			
2g	generalization			
3	/d/			
3g	generalization			
4	/h/			
4g	generalization			
5	/p/			
5g	generalization			
6	/b/			
6g	generalization			
7	/t/			
7g	generalization			
8	/g/			
8g	generalization			
9	/n/			
9g	generalization			

Child Name: . . . .

Uses Different Words to Request

Teaching Procedure: This program should be taught with reinforcing items. Present the reinforcing item and follow the steps below. The direction is the presence of the reinforcing item.

Prompt Hierarchy: Use the least intrusive prompt required in order for the child to be successful (no prompt, faded verbal, verbal).

Materials: Highly motivating items that the child will want to request.

program started:		program mastered:		
	STEPS	**STARTED**	**MASTERED**	**COMMENTS**
1	I want			
1g	generalization			
2	Can I have			
2g	generalization			
3	Give me please			
3g	generalization			
4	I need			
4g	generalization			

Intraverbal Programs

Child Name: . . . .

Common Animal Intraverbals

Teaching Procedure: Present the child with the direction "A _____ [FILL IN ANIMAL] SAYS _____."

Prompt Hierarchy: Use the least intrusive prompt required in order for the child to be successful (no prompt, faded verbal, verbal).

Materials: None.

Note: Take into account your child's response time before providing a prompt.

program started:		program mastered:		
	STEPS	**STARTED**	**MASTERED**	**COMMENTS**
1	dog (woof or bark)			
1g	generalization			
2	cat (meow)			
2g	generalization			
3	cow (moo)			
3g	generalization			
4	pig (oink)			
4g	generalization			
5	horse (neigh)			
5g	generalization			
6	lion (roar)			
6g	generalization			
7	bear (grrrr)			
7g	generalization			
8	monkey (ooo ooo ah ah)			
8g	generalization			
9	bird (chirp)			
9g	generalization			

Child Name: . . . .

Common Intraverbals

Teaching Procedure: Present the child with the first part of the fill-in and wait for the child to respond. For example in step 1: up and ___ (wait for child to say "down").

Prompt Hierarchy: Use the least intrusive prompt required in order for the child to be successful (no prompt, faded verbal, verbal).

Materials: None.

Note: Take into account your child's response time before providing a prompt.

program started:		program mastered:		
	STEPS	STARTED	MASTERED	COMMENTS
1	up and ___ (down)			
1g	generalization			
2	ready, set, ___ (go)			
2g	generalization			
3	1, 2, ___ (3)			
3g	generalization			
4	Winnie the ___ (Pooh)			
4g	generalization			
5	follow the ___ (leader)			
5g	generalization			
6	peek a ___ (boo)			
6g	generalization			
7	hide and ___ (seek)			
7g	generalization			
8	let's go ___ (play)			
8g	generalization			
9	go down the ___ (slide)			
9g	generalization			

Child Name: . . . .

Daily Activity Intraverbals

Teaching Procedure: Present the child with the question in each step. For example in step 1: "You wash your ___."

Prompt Hierarchy: Use the least intrusive prompt required in order for the child to be successful (no prompt, faded verbal, verbal).

Materials: None.

Note: Take into account your child's response time before providing a prompt.

program started:		program mastered:		
	STEPS	**STARTED**	**MASTERED**	**COMMENTS**
1	wash your ___ (hands)			
1g	generalization			
2	zip your ___ (jacket/coat)			
2g	generalization			
3	put on your ___ (shoes)			
3g	generalization			
4	brush your ___ (hair)			
4g	generalization			
5	sleep in a ___ (bed)			
5g	generalization			
6	you eat ___ (food)			
6g	generalization			
7	read the ___ (book)			
7g	generalization			
8	play with the ___ (toys)			
8g	generalization			
9	talk on the ___ (phone)			
9g	generalization			

Child Name: . . . .

Social Questions

Teaching Procedure: Present the child with the direction: ASK THE CHILD THE QUESTION IN EACH STEP. For example in step 1: "What is your name?"

Prompt Hierarchy: Use the least intrusive prompt required in order for the child to be successful (no prompt, faded verbal, verbal).

Materials: None.

Note: Take into account your child's response time before providing a prompt.

program started:		program mastered:		
	STEPS	**STARTED**	**MASTERED**	**COMMENTS**
1	name			
1g	generalization			
2	age			
2g	generalization			
3	names(s) of sibling(s)			
3g	generalization			
4	mom's name			
4g	generalization			
5	address			
5g	generalization			
6	city/town you live in			
6g	generalization			
7	state you live in			
7g	generalization			
8	telephone number			
8g	generalization			

Play Programs

Child Name: . . . .

Single Piece Puzzle

Teaching Procedure: Present the child with the direction "DO PUZZLE."

Prompt Hierarchy: Use the least intrusive prompt required in order for the child to be successful (no prompt, gestural, faded physical, physical).

Materials: Single piece puzzles.

Note: Use a backward chaining procedure.

program started:		program mastered		
	STEPS	STARTED	MASTERED	COMMENTS
1	instructor completes all puzzle pieces EXCEPT the last 1			
1g	generalization			
2	instructor completes all puzzle pieces EXCEPT the last 2			
2g	generalization			
3	instructor completes all puzzle pieces EXCEPT the last 3			
3g	generalization			
4	instructor completes all puzzle pieces EXCEPT the last 4			
4g	generalization			

Child Name: . . . .

Shape Sorter

Teaching Procedure: Present the child with the direction "PLAY WITH THE SHAPE SORTER" and follow steps below.

Prompt Hierarchy: Use the least intrusive prompt required in order for the child to be successful (no prompt, gestural, faded physical, physical).

Materials: Shape sorter.

program started:		program mastered:		
	STEPS	**STARTED**	**MASTERED**	**COMMENTS**
1	the child will place the circle in (or whatever shape you choose)			
1g	generalization (circle)			
2	the child will place the oval in (or whatever shape you choose)			
2g	generalization (both circle and oval)			
3	the child will place the square in (or whatever shape you choose)			
3g	generalization (circle, oval, and square)			
4	the child will place the triangle in (or whatever shape you choose)			
4g	generalization (circle, oval, square, and triangle)			
5	the child will place the rectangle in (or whatever shape you choose)			
5g	generalization (circle, oval, square, triangle, and rectangle)			
6	the child will place the star in (or whatever shape you choose)			
6g	generalization (circle, oval, square, triangle, rectangle, and star)			

Child Name: . . . .

Plays By Self

Teaching Procedure: Present the child with the direction "GO PLAY."

Prompt Hierarchy: Use the least intrusive prompt required in order for the child to be successful (no prompt, gesture, faded physical, physical).

Materials: Toys the child is able to play with by themselves.

program started:		program mastered:		
	STEPS	**STARTED**	**MASTERED**	**COMMENTS**
1	30 seconds			
1g	generalization			
2	1 minute			
2g	generalization			
3	3 minutes			
3g	generalization			
4	5 minutes			
4g	generalization			
5	up to 10 minutes			
5g	generalization			

Child Name: . . . .

Various Methods of Play

Teaching Procedure: Present the child with the direction: STATE ACTION IN EACH STEP [E.G. BOUNCE BALL].

Prompt Hierarchy: Use the least intrusive prompt required in order for the child to be successful (no prompt, gestural, faded physical, physical).

Materials: Various balls, various cars, brush, doll, cup, spoon, baby doll, car ramp, car tunnel, dog.

Note: Generalization should involve changing the direction to "play with [object]" and having the child demonstrate mastery of various methods of play.

program started:		program mastered:		
	STEPS	**STARTED**	**MASTERED**	**COMMENTS**
1	bounce ball			
1g	generalization			
2	roll ball			
2g	generalization			
3	throw ball			
3g	generalization			
4	kick ball			
4g	generalization			
5	make car go in a circle			
5g	generalization			
6	push car down ramp			
6g	generalization			

7	make car go through tunnel			
7g	generalization			
8	brush own hair			
8g	generalization			
9	brush doll hair			
9g	generalization			
10	brush teacher/parent hair			
10g	generalization			
11	drink from a cup			
11g	generalization			
12	pour water into a cup			
12g	generalization			
13	stir spoon in cup			
13g	generalization			
14	give baby a drink from the cup			
14g	generalization			

Child Name: . . . .

Ball Play

Teaching Procedure: Present the child with the direction "LET'S PLAY WITH THE BALL [THEN STATE THE ACTION YOU WANT THE CHILD TO PERFORM]." Example (step 1): "let's play with the ball, let's roll it back and forth."

Prompt Hierarchy: Use the least intrusive prompt required in order for the child to be successful (no prompt, gesture, faded physical, physical).

Materials: Ball.

program started:		program mastered:		
	STEPS	**STARTED**	**MASTERED**	**COMMENTS**
1	roll a ball back and forth			
1g	generalization			
2	roll the ball and knock down pins			
2g	generalization			
3	kick a ball back and forth			
3g	generalization			
4	kick a ball into a goal			
4g	generalization			
5	throw a ball back and forth			
5g	generalization			
6	throw a ball at a target			
6g	generalization			

Child Name:. . . . .

Plays with Indoor Toys

Teaching Procedure: Present the child with the direction "PLAY WITH ___ [TOY]."

Prompt Hierarchy: Use the least intrusive prompt required in order for the child to be successful (no prompt, gesture, faded physical, physical).

Materials: Shape sorter, pop-up toy, puzzle, doll/action hero.

Note: Suggested toys are provided; however, use toys that are in the child's home.

program started:		program mastered:		
	STEPS	**STARTED**	**MASTERED**	**COMMENTS**
1	shape sorter			
1g	generalization			
2	pop-up toy			
2g	generalization			
3	puzzle			
3g	generalization			
4	doll/action hero			
4g	generalization			
5	cars			
5g	generalization			

Child Name: . . . .

Outdoor Play

Teaching Procedure: Present the child with the direction "PLAY WITH/ON _____."

Prompt Hierarchy: Use the least intrusive prompt required in order for the child to be successful (no prompt, gesture, faded physical, physical).

Materials: Slide, swing, chalk, ball.

program started:		program mastered:		
	STEPS	STARTED	MASTERED	COMMENTS
1	goes on slide			
1g	generalization			
2	goes on swing			
2g	generalization			
3	plays with chalk			
3g	generalization			
4	plays with a ball			
4g	generalization			

Child Name: . . . .

Uses Language While Playing

Teaching Procedure: Present the child with the direction: "PLAY."

Prompt Hierarchy: Use the least intrusive prompt required in order for the child to be successful (no prompt, faded verbal, verbal).

Materials: Toys that the child is able to play with independently.

Note: Try to use toys like a car so the child can say "vroom"; or for a train, "choo choo."

program started:		program mastered:		
	STEPS	**STARTED**	**MASTERED**	**COMMENTS**
1	uses at least 1 word for 1 toy			
1g	generalization			
2	uses at least 2 words for 1 toy			
2g	generalization			
3	uses at least 3 words for 1 toy			
3g	generalization			
4	uses at least 3 words for 2 different toys			
4g	generalization			
5	uses at least 5 words for 3 different toys			
5g	generalization			

Child Name: . . . .

Sings Songs

Teaching Procedure: Present the child with the direction "LET'S SING _____ [NAME SONG]."

Prompt Hierarchy: Use the least intrusive prompt required in order for the child to be successful (for non-verbal prompting—no prompt, gesture, faded physical, physical; for verbal prompting—no prompt, faded verbal, verbal) depending on whether you are teaching the hand movements or the words.

Materials: None.

program started:		program mastered:		
	STEPS	STARTED	MASTERED	COMMENTS
1	Itsy Bitsy Spider—hand movements only			
1a	Itsy Bitsy Spider—words if the child is verbal			
1g	generalization			
2	If You're Happy and You Know It—hand movements only			
2a	If You're Happy and You Know It—words if the child is verbal			
2g	generalization			
3	Head, Shoulder, Knees, and Toes—hand movements only			
3a	Head, Shoulder, Knees, and Toes—words if the child is verbal			
3g	generalization			

Child Name: . . . .

Games

Teaching Procedure: Present the child with the direction "LET'S PLAY ___ [NAME THE GAME]."

Prompt Hierarchy: Use the least intrusive prompt required in order for the child to be successful (for non-verbal prompting—no prompt, gesture, faded physical, physical; for verbal prompting—no prompt, faded verbal, verbal).

Materials: None.

Note: You need to teach both the words and actions with each step of duck duck goose. If the child is not verbal, then teach just the actions for both duck duck goose and ring around the rosy.

program started:		program mastered:		
	STEPS	**STARTED**	**MASTERED**	**COMMENTS**
1	duck duck goose			
1a	child sits while someone else gets picked as the goose			
1b	child is picked as the goose			
1c	child gets to be the one that walks around the circle and chooses the goose			
1g	generalization			
2	ring around the rosy			
2a	practice just the motions			
2b	learn the words			
2g	generalization			

Child Name:. . . . .

Pretend Play

Teaching Procedure: Present the child with the direction "LET'S BE A ___ [NAME CHARACTER]."

Prompt Hierarchy: Use the least intrusive prompt required in order for the child to be successful (no prompt, gesture, faded physical, physical).

Materials: Dress-up clothes of a policeman, fireman, princess, doctor, etc.

Note: Child will need to dress up like the character and act like them too.

program started:		program mastered:		
	STEPS	STARTED	MASTERED	COMMENTS
1	policeman			
1g	generalization			
2	fireman			
2g	generalization			
3	doctor			
3g	generalization			
4	princess/action hero			
4g	generalization			

Self Help Programs

Child Name: . . . .

Drinks from a Cup

Teaching Procedure: Present the child with the direction "DRINK/TAKE A SIP."

Prompt Hierarchy: Use the MOST intrusive prompt required in order for the child to be successful (no prompt, gesture, physical, faded physical).

Materials: Cup with highly preferred liquid in it.

Note: When the child is on step 3, initially you will want to prompt the child so that they do not pour too much liquid into their mouth. In this situation, please use a physical prompt and systematically fade your prompts to ensure success.

program started:		program mastered:		
	STEPS	**STARTED**	**MASTERED**	**COMMENTS**
1	will pick up the cup with 2 hands			
1g	generalization			
2	will put the cup to their mouth			
2g	generalization			
3	will take 1 sip out of the cup			
3g	generalization			
4	will put the cup back down			
4g	generalization			

Child Name: . . . .

Uses a Spoon

Teaching Procedure: Present the child with the direction "EAT."

Prompt Hierarchy: Use the least intrusive prompt required in order for the child to be successful (no prompt, gesture, faded physical, physical).

Materials: Spoon, bowl, highly preferred edible that is easy to scoop up (yogurt, oatmeal).

program started:		program mastered:		
	STEPS	STARTED	MASTERED	COMMENTS
1	will pick up the spoon			
1g	generalization			
2	will take the spoon and scoop up the food			
2g	generalization			
3	will take the spoon and put it in their mouth			
3g	generalization			
4	will put the spoon down			
4g	generalization			

Child Name:. . . . .

Uses a Fork

Teaching Procedure: Present the child with the direction "EAT."

Prompt Hierarchy: Use the least intrusive prompt required in order for the child to be successful (no prompt, gesture, faded physical, physical).

Materials: Fork, highly preferred edible that is easy to stab with a fork.

program started:		program mastered:		
	STEPS	**STARTED**	**MASTERED**	**COMMENTS**
1	will pick up the fork			
1g	generalization			
2	will take the fork and stab the edible			
2g	generalization			
3	will take the fork and put it in their mouth			
3g	generalization			
4	will put the fork down			
4g	generalization			

Child Name:. . . . .

Getting Dressed: Shoes

Teaching Procedure: Present the child with the direction: "PUT SHOES ON/TAKE SHOES OFF."

Prompt Hierarchy: Use the least intrusive prompt required in order for the child to be successful (no prompt, gesture, faded physical, physical).

Materials: Shoes.

Note: Only work with Velcro shoes.

program started:		program mastered:		
	STEPS	STARTED	MASTERED	COMMENTS
1	can pull open the Velcro			
1g	generalization			
2	can take shoes off			
2g	generalization			
3	can put shoes on			
3g	generalization			
4	can close the Velcro			
4g	generalization			

Child Name: . . . .

Getting Dressed: Pants

Teaching Procedure: Present the child with the direction "PUT PANTS ON/TAKE PANTS OFF."

Prompt Hierarchy: Use the least intrusive prompt required in order for the child to be successful (no prompt, gesture, faded physical, physical).

Materials: Pants.

Note: The child does not need to zipper or button the pants.

program started:		program mastered:		
	STEPS	STARTED	MASTERED	COMMENTS
1	can pull pants down			
1g	generalization			
2	can pull pants down and take both feet out			
2g	generalization			
3	can pull pants up			
3g	generalization			
4	can put both feet in the pants and pull them up			
4g	generalization			

Child Name: . . . .

Getting Dressed: Shirt

Teaching Procedure: Present the child with the direction "PUT SHIRT ON/TAKE SHIRT OFF."

Prompt Hierarchy: Use the least intrusive prompt required in order for the child to be successful (no prompt, gesture, faded physical, physical).

Materials: Shirt.

program started:		program mastered:		
	STEPS	**STARTED**	**MASTERED**	**COMMENTS**
1	can pull right arm out of sleeve			
1g	generalization			
2	can pull left arm out of sleeve			
2g	generalization			
3	can pull shirt over their head			
3g	generalization			
4	can pull shirt over their head (putting it back on)			
4g	generalization			
5	can put right arm in sleeve			
5g	generalization			
6	can put left arm in sleeve			
6g	generalization			

Child Name: . . . .

Wash Hands

Teaching Procedure: Present the child with the direction "WASH HANDS."

Prompt Hierarchy: Use the least intrusive prompt required in order for the child to be successful (no prompt, gesture, faded physical, physical).

Materials: Sink, soap.

Note: This program should be taught using backwards chaining. This means that you will physically prompt the child through the entire sequence up until the last step. Once the last step is mastered, you will prompt the child through the sequence except the last 2 steps. This program is written so step 1 is the last step in the sequence.

program started:		program mastered:		
	STEPS	**STARTED**	**MASTERED**	**COMMENTS**
1	turn off water			
1g	generalization			
2	place both hands under the water until all soap is gone			
2g	generalization			
3	rub left palm to back of right hand			
3g	generalization			
4	rub right palm to back of left hand			
4g	generalization			
5	rub palms together			
5g	generalization			
6	get soap			
6g	generalization			
7	place hands under the water			
7g	generalization			
8	turn on cold water			
8g	generalization			

Child Name: . . . .

Dry Hands

Teaching Procedure: Present the child with the direction "DRY HANDS."

Prompt Hierarchy: Use the least intrusive prompt required in order for the child to be successful (no prompt, gesture, faded physical, physical).

Materials: Towel.

Note: This program should be taught using backwards chaining. This means that you will physically prompt the child through the entire sequence up until the last step. Once the last step is mastered, you will prompt the child through the sequence except the last 2 steps. This program is written so step 1 is the last step in the sequence.

program started:		program mastered:		
	STEPS	**STARTED**	**MASTERED**	**COMMENTS**
1	throw out towel			
1g	generalization			
2	dry the back of the right hand			
2g	generalization			
3	dry the back of the left hand			
3g	generalization			
4	dry the palms of both hands			
4g	generalization			
5	get paper towel			
5g	generalization			

Sort/Match Programs

Child Name: . . . .

Match Identical Picture to Picture

Teaching Procedure: Present the child with the direction "MATCH" and follow the steps below.

Prompt Hierarchy: Use the least intrusive prompt required in order for the child to be successful (no prompt, gestural, faded physical, physical).

Materials: Any common picture to picture can be used. Some suggestions are: car, animal, plate, utensils, clothing, brush, cup, book.

Note: Example of step 2 (match 2 different pictures to pictures in a field of 2). Lay down a picture of a cow and a car. Present the child with 2 pictures (1 of a cow and 1 of a car). Tell the child to match.

program started:		program mastered:		
	STEPS	**STARTED**	**MASTERED**	**COMMENTS**
1	will match a picture to picture in a field of 1			
1g	generalization—1 picture to picture in a field of 1 with 3 different people in 3 different settings			
2	will match 2 different pictures to pictures in a field of 2			
2g	generalization—up to 2 different pictures to pictures in a field of 2 with 3 different people in 3 different settings			
3	will match 3 different pictures to pictures in a field of 3			
3g	generalization—up to 3 different pictures to pictures in a field of 3 or more with 3 different people in 3 different settings			
4	will match up to 4 different pictures to pictures in a field of 3 or more			
4g	generalization—up to 4 different pictures to pictures in a field of 3 or more with 3 different people in 3 different settings			

5	will match up to 5 different pictures to pictures in a field of 3 or more			
5g	generalization—up to 5 different pictures to pictures in a field of 3 or more with 3 different people in 3 different settings			
6	will match up to 6 different pictures to pictures in a field of 3 or more			
6g	generalization—up to 6 different pictures to pictures in a field of 3 or more with 3 different people in 3 different settings			
7	will match up to 7 different pictures to pictures in a field of 3 or more			
7g	generalization—up to 7 different pictures to pictures in a field of 3 or more with 3 different people in 3 different settings			
8	will match up to 8 different pictures to pictures in a field of 3 or more			
8g	generalization—up to 8 different pictures to pictures in a field of 3 or more with 3 different people in 3 different settings			
9	will match up to 9 different pictures to pictures in a field of 3 or more			
9g	generalization—up to 9 different pictures to pictures in a field of 3 or more with 3 different people in 3 different settings			
10	will match up to 10 different pictures to pictures in a field of 3 or more			
10g	generalization—up to 10 different pictures to pictures in a field of 3 or more with 3 different people in 3 different settings			

Child Name: . . . .

Match Identical Object to Object

Teaching Procedure: Present the child with the direction "MATCH" and follow the steps below.

Prompt Hierarchy: Use the least intrusive prompt required in order for the child to be successful (no prompt, gestural, faded physical, physical).

Materials: Any common object to object can be used. Some suggestions are: car, animal, plate, utensils, clothing, brush, cup, book.

Note: Example of step 2 (match 2 different objects to objects in a field of 2). Lay down an object of a cow and a car. Present the child with 2 objects (1 a cow and 1 of a car). Tell the child to match.

program started:		program mastered:		
	STEPS	**STARTED**	**MASTERED**	**COMMENTS**
1	will match an object to object in a field of 1			
1g	generalization—1 object to object in a field of 1 with 3 different people in 3 different settings			
2	will match 2 different objects to objects in a field of 2			
2g	generalization—up to 2 different objects to objects in a field of 2 with 3 different people in 3 different settings			
3	will match 3 different objects to objects in a field of 3			
3g	generalization—up to 3 different objects to objects in a field of 3 or more with 3 different people in 3 different settings			
4	will match up to 4 different objects to objects in a field of 3 or more			
4g	generalization—up to 4 different objects to objects in a field of 3 or more with 3 different people in 3 different settings			
5	will match up to 5 different objects to objects in a field of 3 or more			

5g	generalization—up to 5 different objects to objects in a field of 3 or more with 3 different people in 3 different settings			
6	will match up to 6 different objects to objects in a field of 3 or more			
6g	generalization—up to 6 different objects to objects in a field of 3 or more with 3 different people in 3 different settings			
7	will match up to 7 different objects to objects in a field of 3 or more			
7g	generalization—up to 7 different objects to objects in a field of 3 or more with 3 different people in 3 different settings			
8	will match up to 8 different objects to objects in a field of 3 or more			
8g	generalization—up to 8 different objects to objects in a field of 3 or more with 3 different people in 3 different settings			
9	will match up to 9 different objects to objects in a field of 3 or more			
9g	generalization—up to 9 different objects to objects in a field of 3 or more with 3 different people in 3 different settings			
10	will match up to 10 different objects to objects in a field of 3 or more			
10g	generalization—up to 10 different objects to objects in a field of 3 or more with 3 different people in 3 different settings			

Child Name: . . . .

Match Object to Picture

Teaching Procedure: Present the child with the direction: "MATCH" and follow the steps below.

Prompt Hierarchy: Use the least intrusive prompt required in order for the child to be successful (no prompt, gestural, faded physical, physical).

Materials: You will need common objects that correspond to the same pictures. Some examples are: car, animal, furniture, ball, crayon, utensil, clothing.

Note: Example of step 2 (match 2 different objects to pictures in a field of 2). Lay down a picture of a cow and a car. Present the child with 2 objects (1 a cow and 1 a car). Tell the child to match.

program started:		program mastered:		
	STEPS	**STARTED**	**MASTERED**	**COMMENTS**
1	will match an object to a picture in a field of 1			
1g	generalization—1 object to a picture in a field of 1 with 3 different people in 3 different settings			
2	will match 2 different objects to pictures in a field of 2			
2g	generalization—up to 2 different objects to pictures in a field of 2 with 3 different people in 3 different settings			
3	will match 3 different objects to pictures in a field of 3			
3g	generalization—up to 3 different objects to pictures in a field of 3 or more with 3 different people in 3 different settings			
4	will match up to 4 different objects to pictures in a field of 3 or more			
4g	generalization—up to 4 different objects to pictures in a field of 3 or more with 3 different people in 3 different settings			

5	will match up to 5 different objects to pictures in a field of 3 or more			
5g	generalization—up to 5 different objects to pictures in a field of 3 or more with 3 different people in 3 different settings			
6	will match up to 6 different objects to pictures in a field of 3 or more			
6g	generalization—up to 6 different objects in a field of 3 or more with 3 different people in 3 different settings			
7	will match up to 7 different objects to pictures in a field of 3 or more			
7g	generalization—up to 7 different objects to pictures in a field of 3 or more with 3 different people in 3 different settings			
8	will match up to 8 different objects to pictures in a field of 3 or more			
8g	generalization—up to 8 different objects in a field of 3 or more with 3 different people in 3 different settings			
9	will match up to 9 different objects to pictures in a field of 3 or more			
9g	generalization—up to 9 different objects in a field of 3 or more with 3 different people in 3 different settings			
10	will match up to 10 different objects to pictures in a field of 3 or more			
10g	generalization—up to 10 different objects to pictures in a field of 3 or more with 3 different people in 3 different settings			

Child Name: . . . .

Sort Identical Items

Teaching Procedure: For steps 1–5: lay down 3 non-identical items but all from the same category (e.g. colors); give the child the matching items and ask them to sort. For example, lay down purple, red, and blue on the table. Give the child 2 purples, 2 reds, and 2 blues (at least 2) and ask them to sort. For step 6: lay down on table at least 3 different categories (clothing, utensil, shape) and give the child at least 2 items from each category and ask them to sort. For example, on the table is a shoe, fork, and square. Give the child 2 shoes, 2 forks, and 2 squares and tell them to sort.

Prompt Hierarchy: Use the least intrusive prompt required in order for the child to be successful (no prompt, gesture, faded physical, physical).

Materials: Same exact animals, utensils, colors, shapes, clothes.

program started:		program mastered:		
	STEPS	**STARTED**	**MASTERED**	**COMMENTS**
1	in a field of 3 can sort identical colors (e.g. red to red, blue to blue, purple to purple)			
1g	generalization			
2	in a field of 3 can sort identical animals (e.g. tiger to tiger, lion to lion, dog to dog)			
2g	generalization			
3	in a field of 3 can sort identical shapes			
3g	generalization			
4	in a field of 3 can sort identical utensils			
4g	generalization			
5	in a field of 3 can sort identical articles of clothing			
5g	generalization			
6	in a field of 3 or more, sort identical items from different categories			
6g	generalization			

Child Name:. . . . .

Sort Non-Identical Items

Teaching Procedure: Lay down 3 (or more, depending on the step) non-identical items: car, color, article of clothing. Present the child with 2 or more items from each category and ask them to sort. The items should be from the same category but not identical items. For example, car, blue, and shirt are on the table. Give the child 2 (or more) non-identical vehicles, 2 (or more) colors, and 2 (or more) articles of clothing and tell the child to sort.

Prompt Hierarchy: Use the least intrusive prompt required in order for the child to be successful (no prompt, gesture, faded physical, physical).

Materials: Animals, utensils, colors, shapes, clothes, books, dolls, cars.

program started:		program mastered:		
	STEPS	**STARTED**	**MASTERED**	**COMMENTS**
1	in a field of 3 can sort non-identical items			
1g	generalization			
2	in a field of 5 can sort non-identical items			
2g	generalization			
3	in a field of 8 can sort non-identical items			
3g	generalization			

Academic Programs

Child Name: . . . .

Receptive Identification of Colors

Teaching Procedure: In a field of 3 or more ask the child to "POINT/TOUCH/SHOW ME ____ [NAME THE COLOR]."

Prompt Hierarchy: Use the least intrusive prompt required in order for the child to be successful (no prompt, gesture, faded physical, physical).

Materials: Various colors on different backgrounds.

program started:		program mastered:		
	STEPS	**STARTED**	**MASTERED**	**COMMENTS**
1	blue			
1g	generalization			
2	green			
2g	generalization			
3	red			
3g	generalization			
4	purple			
4g	generalization			
5	orange			
5g	generalization			
6	yellow			
6g	generalization			
7	brown			
7g	generalization			
8	black			
8g	generalization			
9	white			
9g	generalization			
10	pink			
10g	generalization			

Child Name: . . . .

Expressive Identification of Colors

Teaching Procedure: Hold up the color and ask the child "WHAT IS IT?"

Prompt Hierarchy: Use the least intrusive prompt required in order for the child to be successful (no prompt, faded verbal, verbal).

Materials: Various colors.

program started:		program mastered:		
	STEPS	STARTED	MASTERED	COMMENTS
1	blue			
1g	generalization			
2	green			
2g	generalization			
3	red			
3g	generalization			
4	purple			
4g	generalization			
5	orange			
5g	generalization			
6	yellow			
6g	generalization			
7	brown			
7g	generalization			
8	black			
8g	generalization			
9	white			
9g	generalization			
10	pink			
10g	generalization			

Child Name:. . . . .

Receptive Identification of Shapes

Teaching Procedure: In a field of 3 or more ask the child to "POINT/TOUCH/SHOW ME ___ [NAME THE SHAPE]."

Prompt Hierarchy: Use the least intrusive prompt required in order for the child to be successful (no prompt, gesture, faded physical, physical).

Materials: Various shapes on different backgrounds.

program started:		program mastered:		
	STEPS	**STARTED**	**MASTERED**	**COMMENTS**
1	circle			
1g	generalization			
2	square			
2g	generalization			
3	triangle			
3g	generalization			
4	rectangle			
4g	generalization			
5	oval			
5g	generalization			
6	star			
6g	generalization			

Child Name:. . . . .

Expressive Identification of Shapes

Teaching Procedure: Hold up the shape and ask the child "WHAT SHAPE IS IT?"

Prompt Hierarchy: Use the least intrusive prompt required in order for the child to be successful (no prompt, faded verbal, verbal).

Materials: Various shapes.

program started:		program mastered:		
	STEPS	**STARTED**	**MASTERED**	**COMMENTS**
1	circle			
1g	generalization			
2	square			
2g	generalization			
3	triangle			
3g	generalization			
4	rectangle			
4g	generalization			
5	oval			
5g	generalization			
6	star			
6g	generalization			

Child Name: ....

Receptive Identification of Upper Case Letters

Teaching Procedure: In a field of 3 or more lay out cards/pictures of individual letters; and present the child with the direction: "TOUCH/FIND/POINT TO ___ [LETTER]."

Prompt Hierarchy: Use the least intrusive prompt required in order for the child to be successful (no prompt, gesture, faded physical, physical).

Materials: Various letters in different fonts and colors, and on different types of card.

program started:		STARTED	MASTERED	COMMENTS
	STEPS			
1	A			
1g	generalization			
2	B			
2g	generalization			
3	C			
3g	generalization			
4	D			
4g	generalization			
5	E			
5g	generalization			
6	F			
6g	generalization			
7	G			
7g	generalization			
8	H			
8g	generalization			
9	I			
9g	generalization			
10	J			
10g	generalization			
11	K			
11g	generalization			
12	L			

12g	generalization			
13	M			
13g	generalization			
14	N			
14g	generalization			
15	O			
15g	generalization			
16	P			
16g	generalization			
17	Q			
17g	generalization			
18	R			
18g	generalization			
19	S			
19g	generalization			
20	T			
20g	generalization			
21	U			
21g	generalization			
22	V			
22g	generalization			
23	W			
23g	generalization			
24	X			
24g	generalization			
25	Y			
25g	generalization			
26	Z			
26g	generalization			

Child Name: . . . .

Receptive Identification of Lower Case Letters

Teaching Procedure: In a field of 3 or more lay out cards/pictures of individual letters; and present the child with the direction: "TOUCH/FIND/POINT TO ___ [LETTER]."

Prompt Hierarchy: Use the least intrusive prompt required in order for the child to be successful (no prompt, gesture, faded physical, physical).

Materials: Various letters in different fonts and colors, and on different types of card.

program mastered:				
	STEPS	**STARTED**	**MASTERED**	**COMMENTS**
1	a			
1g	generalization			
2	b			
2g	generalization			
3	c			
3g	generalization			
4	d			
4g	generalization			
5	e			
5g	generalization			
6	f			
6g	generalization			
7	g			
7g	generalization			
8	h			
8g	generalization			
9	i			
9g	generalization			
10	j			
10g	generalization			
11	k			
11g	generalization			
12	l			

12g	generalization			
13	m			
13g	generalization			
14	n			
14g	generalization			
15	o			
15g	generalization			
16	p			
16g	generalization			
17	q			
17g	generalization			
18	r			
18g	generalization			
19	s			
19g	generalization			
20	t			
20g	generalization			
21	u			
21g	generalization			
22	v			
22g	generalization			
23	w			
23g	generalization			
24	x			
24g	generalization			
25	y			
25g	generalization			
26	z			
26g	generalization			

Child Name:. . . . .

Expressive Identification of Upper Case Letters

Teaching Procedure: Hold up a letter card and ask the child "WHAT LETTER IS IT?"

Prompt Hierarchy: Use the least intrusive prompt required in order for the child to be successful (no prompt, faded verbal, verbal).

Materials: Various letters in different fonts and colors, and on different types of card.

program started:		STARTED	MASTERED	COMMENTS
	STEPS			
1	A			
1g	generalization			
2	B			
2g	generalization			
3	C			
3g	generalization			
4	D			
4g	generalization			
5	E			
5g	generalization			
6	F			
6g	generalization			
7	G			
7g	generalization			
8	H			
8g	generalization			
9	I			
9g	generalization			
10	J			
10g	generalization			
11	K			
11g	generalization			
12	L			

12g	generalization			
13	M			
13g	generalization			
14	N			
14g	generalization			
15	O			
15g	generalization			
16	P			
16g	generalization			
17	Q			
17g	generalization			
18	R			
18g	generalization			
19	S			
19g	generalization			
20	T			
20g	generalization			
21	U			
21g	generalization			
22	V			
22g	generalization			
23	W			
23g	generalization			
24	X			
24g	generalization			
25	Y			
25g	generalization			
26	Z			
26g	generalization			

Child Name: ....

Expressive Identification of Lower Case Letters

Teaching Procedure: Hold up a letter card and ask the child "WHAT LETTER IS IT?"

Prompt Hierarchy: Use the least intrusive prompt required in order for the child to be successful (no prompt, faded verbal, verbal).

Materials: Various letters in different fonts and colors, and on different types of card.

program mastered:				
	STEPS	**STARTED**	**MASTERED**	**COMMENTS**
1	a			
1g	generalization			
2	b			
2g	generalization			
3	c			
3g	generalization			
4	d			
4g	generalization			
5	e			
5g	generalization			
6	f			
6g	generalization			
7	g			
7g	generalization			
8	h			
8g	generalization			
9	i			
9g	generalization			
10	j			
10g	generalization			
11	k			
11g	generalization			
12	l			

12g	generalization			
13	m			
13g	generalization			
14	n			
14g	generalization			
15	o			
15g	generalization			
16	p			
16g	generalization			
17	q			
17g	generalization			
18	r			
18g	generalization			
19	s			
19g	generalization			
20	t			
20g	generalization			
21	u			
21g	generalization			
22	v			
22g	generalization			
23	w			
23g	generalization			
24	x			
24g	generalization			
25	y			
25g	generalization			
26	z			
26g	generalization			

Child Name: . . . .

Rote Counting

Teaching Procedure: Present the child with the direction: "COUNT TO ___ [NAME THE NUMBER]."

Prompt Hierarchy: Use the least intrusive prompt required in order for the child to be successful (no prompt, faded verbal, verbal).

Materials: None.

program started:		program mastered:		
	STEPS	STARTED	MASTERED	COMMENTS
1	can count to 5			
1g	generalization			
2	can count to 10			
2g	generalization			
3	can count to 15			
3g	generalization			
4	can count to 20			
4g	generalization			
5	can count to 25			
5g	generalization			
6	can count to 30			
6g	generalization			

Child Name:. . . . .

Counting Objects

Teaching Procedure: Present the child with the direction: "COUNT."

Prompt Hierarchy: Use the least intrusive prompt required in order for the child to be successful (no prompt, faded verbal, verbal).

Materials: Various objects that can be counted.

program started:		program mastered:		
	STEPS	STARTED	MASTERED	COMMENTS
1	can count objects up to 2			
1g	generalization			
2	can count objects up to 3			
2g	generalization			
3	can count objects up to 4			
3g	generalization			
4	can count objects up to 5			
4g	generalization			
5	can count objects up to 6			
5g	generalization			
6	can count objects up to 7			
6g	generalization			
7	can count objects up to 8			
7g	generalization			
8	can count objects up to 9			
8g	generalization			
9	can count objects up to 10			
9g	generalization			

Child Name: . . . .

Receptive Identification of Numbers

Teaching Procedure: In a field of 3 or more present the child with the direction "SHOW ME/POINT TO/TOUCH ___ [NAME THE NUMBER]."

Prompt Hierarchy: Use the least intrusive prompt required in order for the child to be successful (no prompt, gesture, faded physical, physical).

Materials: Cards with numbers on them (use different cards for generalization).

program started:		program mastered:		
	STEPS	**STARTED**	**MASTERED**	**COMMENTS**
1	1			
1g	generalization			
2	2			
2g	generalization			
3	3			
3g	generalization			
4	4			
4g	generalization			
5	5			
5g	generalization			
6	6			
6g	generalization			
7	7			
7g	generalization			
8	8			
8g	generalization			
9	9			
9g	generalization			

10	10			
10g	generalization			
11	11			
11g	generalization			
12	12			
12g	generalization			
13	13			
13g	generalization			
14	14			
14g	generalization			
15	15			
15g	generalization			
16	16			
16g	generalization			
17	17			
17g	generalization			
18	18			
18g	generalization			
19	19			
19g	generalization			
20	20			
20g	generalization			

Child Name: . . . .

Expressive Identification of Numbers

Teaching Procedure: Hold up the number and ask the child "WHAT NUMBER IS IT?"

Prompt Hierarchy: Use the least intrusive prompt required in order for the child to be successful (no prompt, faded verbal, verbal).

Materials: Cards with numbers on them (use different cards for generalization).

program started:		program mastered:		
	STEPS	STARTED	MASTERED	COMMENTS
1	1			
1g	generalization			
2	2			
2g	generalization			
3	3			
3g	generalization			
4	4			
4g	generalization			
5	5			
5g	generalization			
6	6			
6g	generalization			
7	7			
7g	generalization			
8	8			
8g	generalization			
9	9			
9g	generalization			

10	10			
10g	generalization			
11	11			
11g	generalization			
12	12			
12g	generalization			
13	13			
13g	generalization			
14	14			
14g	generalization			
15	15			
15g	generalization			
16	16			
16g	generalization			
17	17			
17g	generalization			
18	18			
18g	generalization			
19	19			
19g	generalization			
20	20			
20g	generalization			

Part III

Mastered Programs

Mastered Program Directions

Purpose

The purpose of this section is to provide an accurate way of keeping continuous data after the child has achieved mastery.

Directions for the Mastered section

Once the child achieves mastery on any step in the program, that step is considered mastered. Ongoing data should be collected to ensure the child does not lose that skill. It is suggested that you collect mastery data twice a month. This section is set up using probe data. This means that you assess the skill: if the child was able to do the skill independently the first time presented then you circle the Y; if the child was not able to demonstrate mastery of the skill the first time it was presented, you circle the N. If the child scored a N, probe the step/program again the next day. If the child receives two consecutive days of N, that step/program goes back into the daily programs until the child reaches the criterion again.

It should also be noted that if a program has steps that build off each other such as quiet hands or hand washing, once the entire program is mastered, it is only necessary to probe the last step. The reason for this is that the last step should include the entire sequence. For example, step 6 in quiet hands is being able to have quiet hands for 1 minute. Therefore, if the child mastered the entire program, we want to make sure the last step is being retained because that includes all the other steps. However, a program such as gross motor imitation, in which the steps do not build off each other, should include probe data for each step once the skill was mastered. Please make sure to include the date in which you probed the skill within that data box.

Generalization in the mastered section

Generalization is included in the steps of the mastered program. It is suggested that this is the step that you collect mastered data on. For example, if the child mastered receptive identification of the color red, collect data on step 3g (red) and not just step 3.

Prompts

This curriculum suggests that you use the prompt that will be the most successful for the child without over-prompting. So if the child is learning a brand new skill, it is probable that they will need a full physical prompt in order to be successful. However, if it is a program for which the child has an 80 percent independent rate, a gestural prompt may be all that is needed. It is also recommended that you fade prompts as quickly as possible so you do not inadvertently promote prompt dependency, as in previous sections.

- *Physical Prompt (P)*—hand-over-hand manipulation

- *Faded Physical Prompt (FP)*—the practitioner is guiding the child

- *Gestural Prompt (G)*—the practitioner points to the correct response

- *Verbal Prompt (VP)**—the answer is verbally provided for the child

- *Faded Verbal Prompt (FV)**—the beginning part of the answer is provided for the child.

Distractors

All programs are designed to be taught in a field of 3 unless otherwise specified; 3 choices are presented to the child—1 being the targeted skill and the other 2 acting as distractors. For example, the child is working on touching the color red. The adult will lay out a picture of a red card, a blue card, and a green card. The blue and green cards will act as distractors.

---

*   A verbal/faded verbal prompt should only be used if you are requiring a verbal response.

Mastered Section Example

Child Name: . . . . Johnny D. . . . .

Quiet Hands

Teaching Procedure: Present the child with the direction "QUIET HANDS OR HANDS DOWN."

Materials: None.

Note: Quiet hands can either be by the child's side or in front of them placed on a table.

	STEPS					
1	child will have quiet hands for 3 seconds	(Y)/N 11/15/10	Y/N	Y/N	Y/N	Y/N
1g	generalization	(Y)/N 11/15/10	Y/N	Y/N	Y/N	Y/N
2	child will have quiet hands for 6 seconds	(Y)/N 12/10/10	Y/N	Y/N	Y/N	Y/N
2g	generalization	(Y)/N 1/3/11	Y/N	Y/N	Y/N	Y/N
3	child will have quiet hands for 10 seconds	(Y)/N 2/15/11	Y/N	Y/N	Y/N	Y/N
3g	generalization	(Y)/N 2/15/11	Y/N	Y/N	Y/N	Y/N
4	child will have quiet hands for 20 seconds	(Y)/N 3/20/11	Y/N	Y/N	Y/N	Y/N
4g	generalization	(Y)/N 3/20/11	Y/N	Y/N	Y/N	Y/N
5	child will have quiet hands for 30 seconds	(Y)/N 5/10/11	Y/N	Y/N	Y/N	Y/N
5g	generalization	(Y)/N 5/10/11	Y/N	Y/N	Y/N	Y/N
6	child will have quiet hands for 1 minute	(Y)/N 7/1/11	Y/N	Y/N	Y/N	Y/N
6g	generalization	(Y)/N 7/1/11	(Y)/N 8/2/11	Y/(N) 8/29/11	(Y)/N 8/30/11	(Y)/N 9/20/11

Note: Please note that quiet hands is a program in which the steps build off each other. Therefore, once the entire program is mastered, it is only necessary to collect data on the last step in the sequence (6g).

Basic Programs

Child Name: . . . .

Quiet Hands

Teaching Procedure: Present the child with the direction "QUIET HANDS OR HANDS DOWN."

Materials: None.

Note: Quiet hands can either be by the child's side or in front of them placed on a table.

	STEPS					
1	child will have quiet hands for 3 seconds	Y/N	Y/N	Y/N	Y/N	Y/N
1g	generalization	Y/N	Y/N	Y/N	Y/N	Y/N
2	child will have quiet hands for 6 seconds	Y/N	Y/N	Y/N	Y/N	Y/N
2g	generalization	Y/N	Y/N	Y/N	Y/N	Y/N
3	child will have quiet hands for 10 seconds	Y/N	Y/N	Y/N	Y/N	Y/N
3g	generalization	Y/N	Y/N	Y/N	Y/N	Y/N
4	child will have quiet hands for 20 seconds	Y/N	Y/N	Y/N	Y/N	Y/N
4g	generalization	Y/N	Y/N	Y/N	Y/N	Y/N
5	child will have quiet hands for 30 seconds	Y/N	Y/N	Y/N	Y/N	Y/N
5g	generalization	Y/N	Y/N	Y/N	Y/N	Y/N
6	child will have quiet hands for 1 minute	Y/N	Y/N	Y/N	Y/N	Y/N
6g	generalization	Y/N	Y/N	Y/N	Y/N	Y/N

Child Name:..

Attending

Teaching Procedure: Present the child with the direction: "SIT QUIET." This means hands on lap/table, feet on floor, and the child is facing the instructor. The child does not need to meet eye to eye with the instructor just as long as the child is facing the instructor and the instructor knows the child is attending.

Materials: None.

	STEPS					
1	child will attend within 10 seconds of the direction being presented	Y/N	Y/N	Y/N	Y/N	Y/N
1g	generalization	Y/N	Y/N	Y/N	Y/N	Y/N
2	child will attend within 5 seconds of the direction being presented	Y/N	Y/N	Y/N	Y/N	Y/N
2g	generalization	Y/N	Y/N	Y/N	Y/N	Y/N
3	child will attend within 3 seconds of the direction being presented	Y/N	Y/N	Y/N	Y/N	Y/N
3g	generalization	Y/N	Y/N	Y/N	Y/N	Y/N

Child Name: . . . .

Responds to Name

Teaching Procedure: Present the child with the direction: PRESENT CHILD'S NAME. Follow the steps.

Materials: None.

	STEPS					
1	will respond to name being called within 5 seconds by looking at the person	Y/N	Y/N	Y/N	Y/N	Y/N
1g	generalization	Y/N	Y/N	Y/N	Y/N	Y/N
2	will respond to name being called within 3 seconds by looking at the person	Y/N	Y/N	Y/N	Y/N	Y/N
2g	generalization	Y/N	Y/N	Y/N	Y/N	Y/N
3	will respond to name being called within 1 second by looking at the person	Y/N	Y/N	Y/N	Y/N	Y/N
3g	generalization	Y/N	Y/N	Y/N	Y/N	Y/N

Child Name:. . . . .

Eye Contact

Teaching Procedure: Present the child with the direction "LOOK AT ME."

Materials: None.

Note: Although there is a direction provided, try to not use any direction. Try to get the child to naturally look at you without adding a verbal direction.

	STEPS					
1	maintains eye contact for first 3 seconds	Y/N	Y/N	Y/N	Y/N	Y/N
1g	generalization	Y/N	Y/N	Y/N	Y/N	Y/N
2	maintains eye contact for first 6 seconds	Y/N	Y/N	Y/N	Y/N	Y/N
2g	generalization	Y/N	Y/N	Y/N	Y/N	Y/N
3	maintains eye contact for first 10 seconds	Y/N	Y/N	Y/N	Y/N	Y/N
3g	generalization	Y/N	Y/N	Y/N	Y/N	Y/N

Child Name:. . . . .

Pointing Program

Teaching Procedure: Present the child with the direction: "POINT TO [NAME OBJECT]" and follow steps below.

Materials: Objects/pictures that the child is familiar with.

	STEPS					
1	will point to item when presented immediately in front of the student within 3 seconds	Y/N	Y/N	Y/N	Y/N	Y/N
1g	generalization	Y/N	Y/N	Y/N	Y/N	Y/N
2	will point to item when presented in a down position within 3 seconds	Y/N	Y/N	Y/N	Y/N	Y/N
2g	generalization	Y/N	Y/N	Y/N	Y/N	Y/N
3	will point to item when presented on the right side position within 3 seconds	Y/N	Y/N	Y/N	Y/N	Y/N
3g	generalization	Y/N	Y/N	Y/N	Y/N	Y/N
4	will point to item when presented on the left side position within 3 seconds	Y/N	Y/N	Y/N	Y/N	Y/N
4g	generalization	Y/N	Y/N	Y/N	Y/N	Y/N

Child Name:. . . . .

Responds to Various Directions to Identify an Object/Picture/Item

Teaching Procedure: Present the child with the direction: STATE THE DIRECTION IN EACH STEP.

Materials: Objects/pictures/items that the child is familiar with.

	STEPS					
1	child will "point to" known object/picture/item	Y/N	Y/N	Y/N	Y/N	Y/N
1g	generalization	Y/N	Y/N	Y/N	Y/N	Y/N
2	child will "touch" known object/picture/item	Y/N	Y/N	Y/N	Y/N	Y/N
2g	generalization	Y/N	Y/N	Y/N	Y/N	Y/N
3	child will "give me" known object/picture/item	Y/N	Y/N	Y/N	Y/N	Y/N
3g	generalization	Y/N	Y/N	Y/N	Y/N	Y/N
4	child will "find" known object/picture/item	Y/N	Y/N	Y/N	Y/N	Y/N
4g	generalization	Y/N	Y/N	Y/N	Y/N	Y/N
5	child will "show me" known object/picture/item	Y/N	Y/N	Y/N	Y/N	Y/N
5g	generalization	Y/N	Y/N	Y/N	Y/N	Y/N
6	child will respond to "where is the" known object/picture/item	Y/N	Y/N	Y/N	Y/N	Y/N
6g	generalization	Y/N	Y/N	Y/N	Y/N	Y/N

Behavior Programs

Child Name: ....

Wait Program

Teaching Procedure: Get child to mand for an item that they want. Then tell the child "you need to wait."

Materials: Strong reinforcers.

Note: A mand is when the child communicates their wants and needs to another person *without* being asked "What do you want?" It can be in the form of a gesture, sign language, picture exchange, or words. The point of manding is to get the child to be able to walk up to another person and be able to "mand" for the item that they want. You can think of a mand as the child demanding or requesting an item.

	STEPS					
1	child will wait for 5 seconds before getting the requested item	Y/N	Y/N	Y/N	Y/N	Y/N
1g	generalization	Y/N	Y/N	Y/N	Y/N	Y/N
2	child will wait for 10 seconds before getting the requested item	Y/N	Y/N	Y/N	Y/N	Y/N
2g	generalization	Y/N	Y/N	Y/N	Y/N	Y/N
3	child will wait for 20 seconds before getting the requested item	Y/N	Y/N	Y/N	Y/N	Y/N
3g	generalization	Y/N	Y/N	Y/N	Y/N	Y/N
4	child will wait for 30 seconds before getting the requested item	Y/N	Y/N	Y/N	Y/N	Y/N
4g	generalization	Y/N	Y/N	Y/N	Y/N	Y/N
5	child will wait for 1 minute before getting the requested item	Y/N	Y/N	Y/N	Y/N	Y/N

5g	generalization	Y/N	Y/N	Y/N	Y/N	Y/N
6	child will wait for 3 minutes before getting the requested item	Y/N	Y/N	Y/N	Y/N	Y/N
6g	generalization	Y/N	Y/N	Y/N	Y/N	Y/N
7	child will wait for 5 minutes before getting the requested item	Y/N	Y/N	Y/N	Y/N	Y/N
7g	generalization	Y/N	Y/N	Y/N	Y/N	Y/N

Child Name:...

Transition

Teaching Procedure: Present the child with the direction: "TIME TO GO TO _____ [NAME ACTIVITY]."

Materials: None.

	STEPS					
1	will transition from a non-preferred activity to a preferred activity	Y/N	Y/N	Y/N	Y/N	Y/N
1g	generalization	Y/N	Y/N	Y/N	Y/N	Y/N
2	will transition from a preferred activity to a preferred activity	Y/N	Y/N	Y/N	Y/N	Y/N
2g	generalization	Y/N	Y/N	Y/N	Y/N	Y/N
3	will transition from a preferred activity to a non-preferred activity	Y/N	Y/N	Y/N	Y/N	Y/N
3g	generalization	Y/N	Y/N	Y/N	Y/N	Y/N
4	will transition from a non-preferred activity to a non-preferred activity	Y/N	Y/N	Y/N	Y/N	Y/N
4g	generalization	Y/N	Y/N	Y/N	Y/N	Y/N

Child Name: . . . .

Desensitization to Touch

Teaching Procedure: Present the child with the direction "GIVE ME A _____."
Materials: None.

	STEPS					
1	high 5	Y/N	Y/N	Y/N	Y/N	Y/N
1g	generalization	Y/N	Y/N	Y/N	Y/N	Y/N
2	pat on the back	Y/N	Y/N	Y/N	Y/N	Y/N
2g	generalization	Y/N	Y/N	Y/N	Y/N	Y/N
3	hug	Y/N	Y/N	Y/N	Y/N	Y/N
3g	generalization	Y/N	Y/N	Y/N	Y/N	Y/N
4	hold hands	Y/N	Y/N	Y/N	Y/N	Y/N
4g	generalization	Y/N	Y/N	Y/N	Y/N	Y/N

Child Name:. . . . .

Desensitization to Dentist

Teaching Procedure: This program will be taught in the home for the first 3 steps, then the program will switch to actually being at the dentist office. Each step will walk you through what should be done and how.

Materials: Toothbrush and a mirror that will fit in the child's mouth, then an actual dental office with a dentist.

Note: When teaching this program, use a highly reinforcing item, and as soon as they complete the task in each step, they get their reinforcer. Example: in step 4, the child goes to the dentist office and sits in the chair. The dentist comes in and says hi; as soon as the dentist leaves say "great job at the dentist, here is your ____ (reinforcer)."

	STEPS					
1	*Let's pretend we are going to the dentist. You (the child) be the dentist first;* let the child just do what they want. You can suggest things for them to do.	Y/N	Y/N	Y/N	Y/N	Y/N
1g	generalization	Y/N	Y/N	Y/N	Y/N	Y/N
2	*Let's pretend we are going to the dentist. It is my (teacher/parent) turn to be the dentist. You (child) sit in the chair and say "ah" or open mouth.*	Y/N	Y/N	Y/N	Y/N	Y/N
2g	generalization	Y/N	Y/N	Y/N	Y/N	Y/N
3	*Let's pretend we are going to the dentist. It is my (teacher/parent) turn to be the dentist. You (child) sit in the chair and say "ah" or open mouth;* then take a toothbrush and put it in their mouth for a couple of seconds. If you can, brush their teeth for a couple of seconds.	Y/N	Y/N	Y/N	Y/N	Y/N
3g	generalization	Y/N	Y/N	Y/N	Y/N	Y/N

4	*It's time to go to the dentist.* This time you will actually go to the dentist office and have the child sit in the dental chair for a couple of seconds. Then end the appointment. The dentist should not actually work on the child. They should be in the room when the child is sitting in the chair though.	Y/N	Y/N	Y/N	Y/N	Y/N
4g	generalization	Y/N	Y/N	Y/N	Y/N	Y/N
5	*It's time to go to the dentist.* Have the child sit in the dental chair and have the dentist just look in their mouth today.	Y/N	Y/N	Y/N	Y/N	Y/N
5g	generalization	Y/N	Y/N	Y/N	Y/N	Y/N
6	*It's time to go to the dentist.* Have the child sit in the dental chair and have the dentist perform the work.	Y/N	Y/N	Y/N	Y/N	Y/N
6g	generalization	Y/N	Y/N	Y/N	Y/N	Y/N

Child Name: . . . .

Desensitization to Doctor

Teaching Procedure: This program will be taught in the home for the first 2 steps, then the program will switch to actually being at the doctor's. Each step will walk you through what should be done and how.

Materials: Kids' doctor's kit, real doctor and doctor office.

Note: When teaching this program, use a highly reinforcing item, and as soon as they complete the task in each step, they get their reinforcer. Example: in step 3, they go to the doctor's office and sit in the exam room. The doctor comes in and says hi; as soon as the doctor leaves say "great job at the doctor, here is your ___ (reinforcer)."

	STEPS					
1	*Let's pretend we are going to the doctor. You (the child) be the doctor first;* let the child just do what they want. You can suggest things for them to do. Make sure you give them the kids' doctor's kit to play with.	Y/N	Y/N	Y/N	Y/N	Y/N
1g	generalization	Y/N	Y/N	Y/N	Y/N	Y/N
2	*Let's pretend we are going to the doctor. It is my (teacher/parent) turn to be the doctor.* Use the kids' doctor's kit and look in the child's ear and throat. Also listen to their chest.	Y/N	Y/N	Y/N	Y/N	Y/N
2g	generalization	Y/N	Y/N	Y/N	Y/N	Y/N
3	*It's time to go to the doctor.* This time you will actually go to the doctor office and have the child sit in the exam room. Have the doctor come in and just say hi. Then end the appointment.	Y/N	Y/N	Y/N	Y/N	Y/N
3g	generalization	Y/N	Y/N	Y/N	Y/N	Y/N
4	*It's time to go to the doctor.* This time the doctor will examine the child.	Y/N	Y/N	Y/N	Y/N	Y/N
4g	generalization	Y/N	Y/N	Y/N	Y/N	Y/N

Child Name: . . . .

Desensitization to Haircuts

Teaching Procedure: Present the child with the direction: "IT'S TIME FOR A HAIRCUT" and follow the steps below.

Materials: Play-doh scissors, smock, hair dresser, hair dresser shop.

Note: Generalization should include other people giving the haircut (until you actually get to the hair dresser, then it should be a consistent hair dresser).

	STEPS					
1	Tell the child: *Let's pretend to get a haircut. You (child) be the hair dresser first.* Tell the child to put a smock on you and then let the child just do what they want.	Y/N	Y/N	Y/N	Y/N	Y/N
1g	generalization	Y/N	Y/N	Y/N	Y/N	Y/N
2	*It's time for a haircut, sit down in the chair. I am going to put a smock on you.* Then just take your hand and start to touch the child's hair. End the haircut here.	Y/N	Y/N	Y/N	Y/N	Y/N
2g	generalization	Y/N	Y/N	Y/N	Y/N	Y/N
3	*It's time for a haircut, sit down in the chair. I am going to put a smock on you.* Then just take your hand and start to touch the child's hair. Then take the play-doh scissors and pretend to cut the child's hair.	Y/N	Y/N	Y/N	Y/N	Y/N
3g	generalization	Y/N	Y/N	Y/N	Y/N	Y/N

4	*It's time for a haircut, let's get in the car.* This time have the child go into the hair dresser and sit in the hair dresser's chair. Let the hair dresser just touch the child's hair and end the haircut at this point. When the child is sitting in the chair, give them something to play with or eat to help distract them. Make sure the toy/food is very reinforcing.	Y/N	Y/N	Y/N	Y/N	Y/N
4g	generalization	Y/N	Y/N	Y/N	Y/N	Y/N
5	*It's time for a haircut, let's get in the car.* This time have the child go into the hair dresser and sit in the hair dresser's chair. Let the hair dresser just touch the child's hair first, then they can start actually cutting the hair. When the child is sitting in the chair, give them something to play with or eat to help distract them. Make sure the toy/food is very reinforcing.	Y/N	Y/N	Y/N	Y/N	Y/N
5g	generalization	Y/N	Y/N	Y/N	Y/N	Y/N

Child Name: . . . .

Clean Up

Teaching Procedure: Have the child play with toys. When finished playing, present the child with the direction "CLEAN UP."

Materials: Toys.

Note: This program is taught using backward chaining. The program can either be taught using 1 toy with many pieces (like a puzzle or Lego) or using more than 1 toy with single pieces (book).

	STEPS					
1	child will pick up the last piece of 1 toy/the last toy	Y/N	Y/N	Y/N	Y/N	Y/N
1g	generalization	Y/N	Y/N	Y/N	Y/N	Y/N
2	child will pick up the last 2 pieces of 1 toy/or the last 2 toys	Y/N	Y/N	Y/N	Y/N	Y/N
2g	generalization	Y/N	Y/N	Y/N	Y/N	Y/N
3	child will pick up the last 3 pieces of 1 toy/or the last 3 toys	Y/N	Y/N	Y/N	Y/N	Y/N
3g	generalization	Y/N	Y/N	Y/N	Y/N	Y/N
4	child will pick up the last 4 pieces of 1 toy/or the remaining 4 toys	Y/N	Y/N	Y/N	Y/N	Y/N
4g	generalization	Y/N	Y/N	Y/N	Y/N	Y/N

Motor Programs

Child Name: . . . .

Gross Motor Imitation

Teaching Procedure: Present the child with the direction: "DO THIS ___."
Materials: None.

	STEPS					
1	clap hands	Y/N	Y/N	Y/N	Y/N	Y/N
1g	generalization	Y/N	Y/N	Y/N	Y/N	Y/N
2	arms up	Y/N	Y/N	Y/N	Y/N	Y/N
2g	generalization	Y/N	Y/N	Y/N	Y/N	Y/N
3	stamp feet	Y/N	Y/N	Y/N	Y/N	Y/N
3g	generalization	Y/N	Y/N	Y/N	Y/N	Y/N
4	tap table	Y/N	Y/N	Y/N	Y/N	Y/N
4g	generalization	Y/N	Y/N	Y/N	Y/N	Y/N
5	arms to side	Y/N	Y/N	Y/N	Y/N	Y/N
5g	generalization	Y/N	Y/N	Y/N	Y/N	Y/N
6	pat tummy	Y/N	Y/N	Y/N	Y/N	Y/N
6g	generalization	Y/N	Y/N	Y/N	Y/N	Y/N
7	rub hands together	Y/N	Y/N	Y/N	Y/N	Y/N
7g	generalization	Y/N	Y/N	Y/N	Y/N	Y/N
8	hand on head	Y/N	Y/N	Y/N	Y/N	Y/N
8g	generalization	Y/N	Y/N	Y/N	Y/N	Y/N
9	arms out in front	Y/N	Y/N	Y/N	Y/N	Y/N
9g	generalization	Y/N	Y/N	Y/N	Y/N	Y/N
10	touch toes	Y/N	Y/N	Y/N	Y/N	Y/N
10g	generalization	Y/N	Y/N	Y/N	Y/N	Y/N

11	stomp 1 foot	Y/N	Y/N	Y/N	Y/N	Y/N
11g	generalization	Y/N	Y/N	Y/N	Y/N	Y/N
12	cross legs sitting	Y/N	Y/N	Y/N	Y/N	Y/N
12g	generalization	Y/N	Y/N	Y/N	Y/N	Y/N
13	lift and hold 1 leg	Y/N	Y/N	Y/N	Y/N	Y/N
13g	generalization	Y/N	Y/N	Y/N	Y/N	Y/N
14	place feet together	Y/N	Y/N	Y/N	Y/N	Y/N
14g	generalization	Y/N	Y/N	Y/N	Y/N	Y/N
15	spread feet apart	Y/N	Y/N	Y/N	Y/N	Y/N
15g	generalization	Y/N	Y/N	Y/N	Y/N	Y/N
16	hop	Y/N	Y/N	Y/N	Y/N	Y/N
16g	generalization	Y/N	Y/N	Y/N	Y/N	Y/N
17	lift foot and shake	Y/N	Y/N	Y/N	Y/N	Y/N
17g	generalization	Y/N	Y/N	Y/N	Y/N	Y/N
18	cross legs standing	Y/N	Y/N	Y/N	Y/N	Y/N
18g	generalization	Y/N	Y/N	Y/N	Y/N	Y/N
19	place foot forward	Y/N	Y/N	Y/N	Y/N	Y/N
19g	generalization	Y/N	Y/N	Y/N	Y/N	Y/N
20	bend side to side at waist	Y/N	Y/N	Y/N	Y/N	Y/N
20g	generalization	Y/N	Y/N	Y/N	Y/N	Y/N
21	shake head yes	Y/N	Y/N	Y/N	Y/N	Y/N
21g	generalization	Y/N	Y/N	Y/N	Y/N	Y/N
22	shake head no	Y/N	Y/N	Y/N	Y/N	Y/N
22g	generalization	Y/N	Y/N	Y/N	Y/N	Y/N
23	move head side to side	Y/N	Y/N	Y/N	Y/N	Y/N
23g	generalization	Y/N	Y/N	Y/N	Y/N	Y/N

Child Name: . . . .

Motor Imitation

Teaching Procedure: Present the child with the direction "DO THIS ___."

Materials: Car, cup, spoon, hammer, doll, drums, bowl, hat.

	STEPS					
1	roll car back and forth	Y/N	Y/N	Y/N	Y/N	Y/N
1g	generalization	Y/N	Y/N	Y/N	Y/N	Y/N
2	drink from a cup	Y/N	Y/N	Y/N	Y/N	Y/N
2g	generalization	Y/N	Y/N	Y/N	Y/N	Y/N
3	stir a spoon in cup	Y/N	Y/N	Y/N	Y/N	Y/N
3g	generalization	Y/N	Y/N	Y/N	Y/N	Y/N
4	bang a hammer	Y/N	Y/N	Y/N	Y/N	Y/N
4g	generalization	Y/N	Y/N	Y/N	Y/N	Y/N
5	feed doll	Y/N	Y/N	Y/N	Y/N	Y/N
5g	generalization	Y/N	Y/N	Y/N	Y/N	Y/N
6	brush hair	Y/N	Y/N	Y/N	Y/N	Y/N
6g	generalization	Y/N	Y/N	Y/N	Y/N	Y/N
7	play drums	Y/N	Y/N	Y/N	Y/N	Y/N
7g	generalization	Y/N	Y/N	Y/N	Y/N	Y/N
8	kiss a doll	Y/N	Y/N	Y/N	Y/N	Y/N
8g	generalization	Y/N	Y/N	Y/N	Y/N	Y/N
9	put object in bowl	Y/N	Y/N	Y/N	Y/N	Y/N
9g	generalization	Y/N	Y/N	Y/N	Y/N	Y/N
10	put hat on	Y/N	Y/N	Y/N	Y/N	Y/N
10g	generalization	Y/N	Y/N	Y/N	Y/N	Y/N

Child Name: ....

Fine Motor Imitation

Teaching Procedure: Present the child with the direction: "DO THIS ___."
Materials: None.

	STEPS					
1	touch thumbs together and hold	Y/N	Y/N	Y/N	Y/N	Y/N
1g	generalization	Y/N	Y/N	Y/N	Y/N	Y/N
2	touch thumb and pointer finger together	Y/N	Y/N	Y/N	Y/N	Y/N
2g	generalization	Y/N	Y/N	Y/N	Y/N	Y/N
3	bounce thumb and pointer finger	Y/N	Y/N	Y/N	Y/N	Y/N
3g	generalization	Y/N	Y/N	Y/N	Y/N	Y/N
4	spread fingers apart	Y/N	Y/N	Y/N	Y/N	Y/N
4g	generalization	Y/N	Y/N	Y/N	Y/N	Y/N
5	touch pointer fingers together	Y/N	Y/N	Y/N	Y/N	Y/N
5g	generalization	Y/N	Y/N	Y/N	Y/N	Y/N
6	touch middle fingers together	Y/N	Y/N	Y/N	Y/N	Y/N
6g	generalization	Y/N	Y/N	Y/N	Y/N	Y/N
7	touch ring fingers together	Y/N	Y/N	Y/N	Y/N	Y/N
7g	generalization	Y/N	Y/N	Y/N	Y/N	Y/N
8	touch pinky fingers together	Y/N	Y/N	Y/N	Y/N	Y/N
8g	generalization	Y/N	Y/N	Y/N	Y/N	Y/N
9	bend fingers down	Y/N	Y/N	Y/N	Y/N	Y/N
9g	generalization	Y/N	Y/N	Y/N	Y/N	Y/N
10	touch thumb and middle finger together	Y/N	Y/N	Y/N	Y/N	Y/N
10g	generalization	Y/N	Y/N	Y/N	Y/N	Y/N

Child Name:. . . . .

Oral Motor Imitation

Teaching Procedure: Present the child with the direction "DO THIS ___."
Materials: None.

	STEPS					
1	open mouth	Y/N	Y/N	Y/N	Y/N	Y/N
1g	generalization	Y/N	Y/N	Y/N	Y/N	Y/N
2	open and close mouth	Y/N	Y/N	Y/N	Y/N	Y/N
2g	generalization	Y/N	Y/N	Y/N	Y/N	Y/N
3	blow (like you are blowing bubbles)	Y/N	Y/N	Y/N	Y/N	Y/N
3g	generalization	Y/N	Y/N	Y/N	Y/N	Y/N
4	lips together and blow (making raspberries with your mouth)	Y/N	Y/N	Y/N	Y/N	Y/N
4g	generalization	Y/N	Y/N	Y/N	Y/N	Y/N
5	stick your tongue out	Y/N	Y/N	Y/N	Y/N	Y/N
5g	generalization	Y/N	Y/N	Y/N	Y/N	Y/N
6	stick your tongue in and out	Y/N	Y/N	Y/N	Y/N	Y/N
6g	generalization	Y/N	Y/N	Y/N	Y/N	Y/N

Child Name: . . . .

Color Between the Lines

Teaching Procedure: Present the child with the direction "COLOR."

Materials: Crayons, paper.

	STEPS					
1	can color a large shape staying within the boundaries approximately 4 square inches or less	Y/N	Y/N	Y/N	Y/N	Y/N
1g	generalization	Y/N	Y/N	Y/N	Y/N	Y/N
2	can color a large shape staying within the boundaries approximately 2 square inches or less	Y/N	Y/N	Y/N	Y/N	Y/N
2g	generalization	Y/N	Y/N	Y/N	Y/N	Y/N

Child Name: ....

Copy Straight Lines

Teaching Procedure: Present the child with the direction "DO THIS."

Materials: Pencil or crayons, paper.

	STEPS					
1	can copy a straight line that is up and down	Y/N	Y/N	Y/N	Y/N	Y/N
1g	generalization	Y/N	Y/N	Y/N	Y/N	Y/N
2	can copy a straight line that is horizontal	Y/N	Y/N	Y/N	Y/N	Y/N
2g	generalization	Y/N	Y/N	Y/N	Y/N	Y/N
3	can copy a diagonal line	Y/N	Y/N	Y/N	Y/N	Y/N
3g	generalization	Y/N	Y/N	Y/N	Y/N	Y/N
4	can copy a square	Y/N	Y/N	Y/N	Y/N	Y/N
4g	generalization	Y/N	Y/N	Y/N	Y/N	Y/N
5	can copy a rectangle	Y/N	Y/N	Y/N	Y/N	Y/N
5g	generalization	Y/N	Y/N	Y/N	Y/N	Y/N
6	can copy a triangle	Y/N	Y/N	Y/N	Y/N	Y/N
6g	generalization	Y/N	Y/N	Y/N	Y/N	Y/N

Receptive Programs

Child Name: . . . .

One Step Directions

Teaching Procedure: Present the child with the direction: STATE THE DIRECTION [E.G. CLAP HANDS]. Follow the steps below.

Materials: None.

	STEPS					
1	clap hands	Y/N	Y/N	Y/N	Y/N	Y/N
1g	generalization	Y/N	Y/N	Y/N	Y/N	Y/N
2	stand up	Y/N	Y/N	Y/N	Y/N	Y/N
2g	generalization	Y/N	Y/N	Y/N	Y/N	Y/N
3	sit down	Y/N	Y/N	Y/N	Y/N	Y/N
3g	generalization	Y/N	Y/N	Y/N	Y/N	Y/N
4	jump	Y/N	Y/N	Y/N	Y/N	Y/N
4g	generalization	Y/N	Y/N	Y/N	Y/N	Y/N
5	wave	Y/N	Y/N	Y/N	Y/N	Y/N
5g	generalization	Y/N	Y/N	Y/N	Y/N	Y/N
6	turn around	Y/N	Y/N	Y/N	Y/N	Y/N
6g	generalization	Y/N	Y/N	Y/N	Y/N	Y/N
7	blow	Y/N	Y/N	Y/N	Y/N	Y/N
7g	generalization	Y/N	Y/N	Y/N	Y/N	Y/N
8	come here	Y/N	Y/N	Y/N	Y/N	Y/N
8g	generalization	Y/N	Y/N	Y/N	Y/N	Y/N
9	stomp feet	Y/N	Y/N	Y/N	Y/N	Y/N
9g	generalization	Y/N	Y/N	Y/N	Y/N	Y/N
10	knock	Y/N	Y/N	Y/N	Y/N	Y/N
10g	generalization	Y/N	Y/N	Y/N	Y/N	Y/N

Child Name: . . . .

Two Step Directions

Teaching Procedure: Present the child with the direction: VERBALLY STATE THE DIRECTIONS [E.G. STAND UP, GET TOY].

Materials: Toy, paper, tissue, garbage, puzzle.

	STEPS					
1	stand up, get toy	Y/N	Y/N	Y/N	Y/N	Y/N
1g	generalization	Y/N	Y/N	Y/N	Y/N	Y/N
2	stand up, turn around	Y/N	Y/N	Y/N	Y/N	Y/N
2g	generalization	Y/N	Y/N	Y/N	Y/N	Y/N
3	get paper, sit down	Y/N	Y/N	Y/N	Y/N	Y/N
3g	generalization	Y/N	Y/N	Y/N	Y/N	Y/N
4	get tissue, wipe your nose	Y/N	Y/N	Y/N	Y/N	Y/N
4g	generalization	Y/N	Y/N	Y/N	Y/N	Y/N
5	wipe your nose, throw out tissue	Y/N	Y/N	Y/N	Y/N	Y/N
5g	generalization	Y/N	Y/N	Y/N	Y/N	Y/N

Child Name: . . . .

Receptive Identification of Pictures

Teaching Procedure: Present the child with the direction: "TOUCH/POINT TO/SHOW ME ___ [NAME PICTURE]."

Materials: Pictures presented in the steps below.

Note: Generalization should include pointing to pictures in books or magazines.

	STEPS					
1	table	Y/N	Y/N	Y/N	Y/N	Y/N
1g	generalization	Y/N	Y/N	Y/N	Y/N	Y/N
2	chair	Y/N	Y/N	Y/N	Y/N	Y/N
2g	generalization	Y/N	Y/N	Y/N	Y/N	Y/N
3	door	Y/N	Y/N	Y/N	Y/N	Y/N
3g	generalization	Y/N	Y/N	Y/N	Y/N	Y/N
4	sink	Y/N	Y/N	Y/N	Y/N	Y/N
4g	generalization	Y/N	Y/N	Y/N	Y/N	Y/N
5	toilet	Y/N	Y/N	Y/N	Y/N	Y/N
5g	generalization	Y/N	Y/N	Y/N	Y/N	Y/N
6	spoon	Y/N	Y/N	Y/N	Y/N	Y/N
6g	generalization	Y/N	Y/N	Y/N	Y/N	Y/N
7	plate	Y/N	Y/N	Y/N	Y/N	Y/N
7g	generalization	Y/N	Y/N	Y/N	Y/N	Y/N
8	book	Y/N	Y/N	Y/N	Y/N	Y/N
8g	generalization	Y/N	Y/N	Y/N	Y/N	Y/N

9	toy	Y/N	Y/N	Y/N	Y/N	Y/N
9g	generalization	Y/N	Y/N	Y/N	Y/N	Y/N
10	crayon	Y/N	Y/N	Y/N	Y/N	Y/N
10g	generalization	Y/N	Y/N	Y/N	Y/N	Y/N
11	paper	Y/N	Y/N	Y/N	Y/N	Y/N
11g	generalization	Y/N	Y/N	Y/N	Y/N	Y/N
12	computer	Y/N	Y/N	Y/N	Y/N	Y/N
12g	generalization	Y/N	Y/N	Y/N	Y/N	Y/N
13	window	Y/N	Y/N	Y/N	Y/N	Y/N
13g	generalization	Y/N	Y/N	Y/N	Y/N	Y/N
14	teddy bear	Y/N	Y/N	Y/N	Y/N	Y/N
14g	generalization	Y/N	Y/N	Y/N	Y/N	Y/N
15	candy	Y/N	Y/N	Y/N	Y/N	Y/N
15g	generalization	Y/N	Y/N	Y/N	Y/N	Y/N
16	camera	Y/N	Y/N	Y/N	Y/N	Y/N
16g	generalization	Y/N	Y/N	Y/N	Y/N	Y/N
17	phone	Y/N	Y/N	Y/N	Y/N	Y/N
17g	generalization	Y/N	Y/N	Y/N	Y/N	Y/N
18	sock	Y/N	Y/N	Y/N	Y/N	Y/N
18g	generalization	Y/N	Y/N	Y/N	Y/N	Y/N
19	shoe	Y/N	Y/N	Y/N	Y/N	Y/N
19g	generalization	Y/N	Y/N	Y/N	Y/N	Y/N

Child Name: . . . .

Receptive Identification of Objects

Teaching Procedure: Present the child with the direction "TOUCH/POINT TO/SHOW ME _____ [NAME OBJECT]."

Materials: Objects presented in the steps below.

	STEPS					
1	sock	Y/N	Y/N	Y/N	Y/N	Y/N
1g	generalization	Y/N	Y/N	Y/N	Y/N	Y/N
2	shoe	Y/N	Y/N	Y/N	Y/N	Y/N
2g	generalization	Y/N	Y/N	Y/N	Y/N	Y/N
3	pencil	Y/N	Y/N	Y/N	Y/N	Y/N
3g	generalization	Y/N	Y/N	Y/N	Y/N	Y/N
4	paper	Y/N	Y/N	Y/N	Y/N	Y/N
4g	generalization	Y/N	Y/N	Y/N	Y/N	Y/N
5	crayon	Y/N	Y/N	Y/N	Y/N	Y/N
5g	generalization	Y/N	Y/N	Y/N	Y/N	Y/N
6	cup	Y/N	Y/N	Y/N	Y/N	Y/N
6g	generalization	Y/N	Y/N	Y/N	Y/N	Y/N
7	camera	Y/N	Y/N	Y/N	Y/N	Y/N
7g	generalization	Y/N	Y/N	Y/N	Y/N	Y/N
8	phone	Y/N	Y/N	Y/N	Y/N	Y/N
8g	generalization	Y/N	Y/N	Y/N	Y/N	Y/N
9	television	Y/N	Y/N	Y/N	Y/N	Y/N

9g	generalization	Y/N	Y/N	Y/N	Y/N	Y/N
10	door	Y/N	Y/N	Y/N	Y/N	Y/N
10g	generalization	Y/N	Y/N	Y/N	Y/N	Y/N
11	toilet	Y/N	Y/N	Y/N	Y/N	Y/N
11g	generalization	Y/N	Y/N	Y/N	Y/N	Y/N
12	sink	Y/N	Y/N	Y/N	Y/N	Y/N
12g	generalization	Y/N	Y/N	Y/N	Y/N	Y/N
13	book	Y/N	Y/N	Y/N	Y/N	Y/N
13g	generalization	Y/N	Y/N	Y/N	Y/N	Y/N
14	balloons	Y/N	Y/N	Y/N	Y/N	Y/N
14g	generalization	Y/N	Y/N	Y/N	Y/N	Y/N
15	table	Y/N	Y/N	Y/N	Y/N	Y/N
15g	generalization	Y/N	Y/N	Y/N	Y/N	Y/N
16	chair	Y/N	Y/N	Y/N	Y/N	Y/N
16g	generalization	Y/N	Y/N	Y/N	Y/N	Y/N
17	teddy bear	Y/N	Y/N	Y/N	Y/N	Y/N
17g	generalization	Y/N	Y/N	Y/N	Y/N	Y/N
18	candy	Y/N	Y/N	Y/N	Y/N	Y/N
18g	generalization	Y/N	Y/N	Y/N	Y/N	Y/N
19	blocks	Y/N	Y/N	Y/N	Y/N	Y/N
19g	generalization	Y/N	Y/N	Y/N	Y/N	Y/N

Child Name: . . . .

Receptive Identification of Body Parts

Teaching Procedure: Present the child with the direction "TOUCH _____ [BODY PART]."

Materials: Dolls, pictures.

Note: Generalization of this program should be touching body parts on other items: other people, dolls, pictures, etc.

	STEPS					
1	nose	Y/N	Y/N	Y/N	Y/N	Y/N
1g	generalization	Y/N	Y/N	Y/N	Y/N	Y/N
2	eyes	Y/N	Y/N	Y/N	Y/N	Y/N
2g	generalization	Y/N	Y/N	Y/N	Y/N	Y/N
3	ears	Y/N	Y/N	Y/N	Y/N	Y/N
3g	generalization	Y/N	Y/N	Y/N	Y/N	Y/N
4	mouth	Y/N	Y/N	Y/N	Y/N	Y/N
4g	generalization	Y/N	Y/N	Y/N	Y/N	Y/N
5	arm	Y/N	Y/N	Y/N	Y/N	Y/N
5g	generalization	Y/N	Y/N	Y/N	Y/N	Y/N
6	leg	Y/N	Y/N	Y/N	Y/N	Y/N
6g	generalization	Y/N	Y/N	Y/N	Y/N	Y/N
7	foot	Y/N	Y/N	Y/N	Y/N	Y/N
7g	generalization	Y/N	Y/N	Y/N	Y/N	Y/N
8	hand	Y/N	Y/N	Y/N	Y/N	Y/N

8g	generalization	Y/N	Y/N	Y/N	Y/N	Y/N
9	elbow	Y/N	Y/N	Y/N	Y/N	Y/N
9g	generalization	Y/N	Y/N	Y/N	Y/N	Y/N
10	knee	Y/N	Y/N	Y/N	Y/N	Y/N
10g	generalization	Y/N	Y/N	Y/N	Y/N	Y/N
11	chin	Y/N	Y/N	Y/N	Y/N	Y/N
11g	generalization	Y/N	Y/N	Y/N	Y/N	Y/N
12	head	Y/N	Y/N	Y/N	Y/N	Y/N
12g	generalization	Y/N	Y/N	Y/N	Y/N	Y/N
13	hair	Y/N	Y/N	Y/N	Y/N	Y/N
13g	generalization	Y/N	Y/N	Y/N	Y/N	Y/N
14	back	Y/N	Y/N	Y/N	Y/N	Y/N
14g	generalization	Y/N	Y/N	Y/N	Y/N	Y/N
15	stomach	Y/N	Y/N	Y/N	Y/N	Y/N
15g	generalization	Y/N	Y/N	Y/N	Y/N	Y/N
16	forehead	Y/N	Y/N	Y/N	Y/N	Y/N
16g	generalization	Y/N	Y/N	Y/N	Y/N	Y/N
17	neck	Y/N	Y/N	Y/N	Y/N	Y/N
17g	generalization	Y/N	Y/N	Y/N	Y/N	Y/N
18	tongue	Y/N	Y/N	Y/N	Y/N	Y/N
18g	generalization	Y/N	Y/N	Y/N	Y/N	Y/N

Child Name: . . . .

Receptive Identification of Articles of Clothing

Teaching Procedure: In a field of 3 or more, lay out the articles of clothing and ask the child to "TOUCH/POINT/SHOW ME _____ [NAME ARTICLE OF CLOTHING]."

Materials: Various articles of clothing including pictures of clothing and actual articles of clothing.

Note: Generalization should include identifying articles of clothing on self and other people, in books, and on dolls.

	STEPS					
1	shirt	Y/N	Y/N	Y/N	Y/N	Y/N
1g	generalization	Y/N	Y/N	Y/N	Y/N	Y/N
2	pants	Y/N	Y/N	Y/N	Y/N	Y/N
2g	generalization	Y/N	Y/N	Y/N	Y/N	Y/N
3	socks	Y/N	Y/N	Y/N	Y/N	Y/N
3g	generalization	Y/N	Y/N	Y/N	Y/N	Y/N
4	shoes	Y/N	Y/N	Y/N	Y/N	Y/N
4g	generalization	Y/N	Y/N	Y/N	Y/N	Y/N
5	underwear/diaper	Y/N	Y/N	Y/N	Y/N	Y/N
5g	generalization	Y/N	Y/N	Y/N	Y/N	Y/N
6	shorts	Y/N	Y/N	Y/N	Y/N	Y/N
6g	generalization	Y/N	Y/N	Y/N	Y/N	Y/N
7	jacket	Y/N	Y/N	Y/N	Y/N	Y/N
7g	generalization	Y/N	Y/N	Y/N	Y/N	Y/N
8	hat	Y/N	Y/N	Y/N	Y/N	Y/N
8g	generalization	Y/N	Y/N	Y/N	Y/N	Y/N
9	gloves	Y/N	Y/N	Y/N	Y/N	Y/N
9g	generalization	Y/N	Y/N	Y/N	Y/N	Y/N

Child Name:. . . . .

Receptive Identification of Familiar People

Teaching Procedure: Present the child with the direction "SHOW ME _____ [NAME THE PERSON]."

Materials: Pictures of people stated below.

Note: Generalization should be the actual person and other pictures of the person, in addition to the child being presented with the picture in different settings and with different people.

	STEPS					
1	mom	Y/N	Y/N	Y/N	Y/N	Y/N
1g	generalization	Y/N	Y/N	Y/N	Y/N	Y/N
2	dad	Y/N	Y/N	Y/N	Y/N	Y/N
2g	generalization	Y/N	Y/N	Y/N	Y/N	Y/N
3	sibling	Y/N	Y/N	Y/N	Y/N	Y/N
3g	generalization	Y/N	Y/N	Y/N	Y/N	Y/N
4	grandmother	Y/N	Y/N	Y/N	Y/N	Y/N
4g	generalization	Y/N	Y/N	Y/N	Y/N	Y/N
5	teacher	Y/N	Y/N	Y/N	Y/N	Y/N
5g	generalization	Y/N	Y/N	Y/N	Y/N	Y/N
6	friend	Y/N	Y/N	Y/N	Y/N	Y/N
6g	generalization	Y/N	Y/N	Y/N	Y/N	Y/N

Child Name: . . . .

Receptive Identification of Emotions

Teaching Procedure: Present the child with the direction "TOUCH ___ [NAME THE EMOTION]."

Materials: Picture cards of the emotions. You can obtain picture cards of emotions through the websites www.do2learn.com and www.difflearn.com. You can also take pictures of yourself demonstrating different emotions.

Note: Generalization should include identifying emotions through pictures, television, books, magazines, and on people.

	STEPS					
1	happy	Y/N	Y/N	Y/N	Y/N	Y/N
1g	generalization	Y/N	Y/N	Y/N	Y/N	Y/N
2	sad	Y/N	Y/N	Y/N	Y/N	Y/N
2g	generalization	Y/N	Y/N	Y/N	Y/N	Y/N
3	angry/mad	Y/N	Y/N	Y/N	Y/N	Y/N
3g	generalization	Y/N	Y/N	Y/N	Y/N	Y/N
4	surprised	Y/N	Y/N	Y/N	Y/N	Y/N
4g	generalization	Y/N	Y/N	Y/N	Y/N	Y/N
5	scared	Y/N	Y/N	Y/N	Y/N	Y/N
5g	generalization	Y/N	Y/N	Y/N	Y/N	Y/N
6	bored	Y/N	Y/N	Y/N	Y/N	Y/N
6g	generalization	Y/N	Y/N	Y/N	Y/N	Y/N
7	embarrassed	Y/N	Y/N	Y/N	Y/N	Y/N
7g	generalization	Y/N	Y/N	Y/N	Y/N	Y/N

Child Name: . . . .

Receptive Identification of Community Helpers

Teaching Procedure: Present the child with the direction: "SHOW ME/POINT TO/TOUCH ____ [COMMUNITY HELPER]."

Materials: Pictures of items below.

	STEPS					
1	policeman	Y/N	Y/N	Y/N	Y/N	Y/N
1g	generalization	Y/N	Y/N	Y/N	Y/N	Y/N
2	fireman	Y/N	Y/N	Y/N	Y/N	Y/N
2g	generalization	Y/N	Y/N	Y/N	Y/N	Y/N
3	mail man	Y/N	Y/N	Y/N	Y/N	Y/N
3g	generalization	Y/N	Y/N	Y/N	Y/N	Y/N
4	doctor	Y/N	Y/N	Y/N	Y/N	Y/N
4g	generalization	Y/N	Y/N	Y/N	Y/N	Y/N
5	nurse	Y/N	Y/N	Y/N	Y/N	Y/N
5g	generalization	Y/N	Y/N	Y/N	Y/N	Y/N
6	bus driver	Y/N	Y/N	Y/N	Y/N	Y/N
6g	generalization	Y/N	Y/N	Y/N	Y/N	Y/N
7	waiter	Y/N	Y/N	Y/N	Y/N	Y/N
7g	generalization	Y/N	Y/N	Y/N	Y/N	Y/N
8	teacher	Y/N	Y/N	Y/N	Y/N	Y/N
8g	generalization	Y/N	Y/N	Y/N	Y/N	Y/N

Child Name: . . . .

Receptive Identification of Environmental Sounds

Teaching Procedure: Present the child with the direction "WHAT SOUND DO YOU HEAR?"
[CHILD WILL POINT/TOUCH THE CORRECT SOUND].

Materials: Sounds of steps below, pictures of steps below.

	STEPS					
1	dog	Y/N	Y/N	Y/N	Y/N	Y/N
1g	generalization	Y/N	Y/N	Y/N	Y/N	Y/N
2	fire truck	Y/N	Y/N	Y/N	Y/N	Y/N
2g	generalization	Y/N	Y/N	Y/N	Y/N	Y/N
3	train	Y/N	Y/N	Y/N	Y/N	Y/N
3g	generalization	Y/N	Y/N	Y/N	Y/N	Y/N
4	horn (on car)	Y/N	Y/N	Y/N	Y/N	Y/N
4g	generalization	Y/N	Y/N	Y/N	Y/N	Y/N
5	airplane	Y/N	Y/N	Y/N	Y/N	Y/N
5g	generalization	Y/N	Y/N	Y/N	Y/N	Y/N
6	ambulance	Y/N	Y/N	Y/N	Y/N	Y/N
6g	generalization	Y/N	Y/N	Y/N	Y/N	Y/N
7	bird	Y/N	Y/N	Y/N	Y/N	Y/N
7g	generalization	Y/N	Y/N	Y/N	Y/N	Y/N
8	telephone ringing	Y/N	Y/N	Y/N	Y/N	Y/N
8g	generalization	Y/N	Y/N	Y/N	Y/N	Y/N
9	door bell	Y/N	Y/N	Y/N	Y/N	Y/N
9g	generalization	Y/N	Y/N	Y/N	Y/N	Y/N
10	baby crying	Y/N	Y/N	Y/N	Y/N	Y/N
10g	generalization	Y/N	Y/N	Y/N	Y/N	Y/N

Expressive Programs

Child Name: . . . .

Expressive Identification of Pictures

Teaching Procedure: Present the child with the direction "WHAT IS THIS? _____ [WHILE HOLDING UP PICTURE/POINTING TO PICTURE]."

Materials: Objects presented in the steps below.

	STEPS					
1	table	Y/N	Y/N	Y/N	Y/N	Y/N
1g	generalization	Y/N	Y/N	Y/N	Y/N	Y/N
2	hair	Y/N	Y/N	Y/N	Y/N	Y/N
2g	generalization	Y/N	Y/N	Y/N	Y/N	Y/N
3	door	Y/N	Y/N	Y/N	Y/N	Y/N
3g	generalization	Y/N	Y/N	Y/N	Y/N	Y/N
4	sink	Y/N	Y/N	Y/N	Y/N	Y/N
4g	generalization	Y/N	Y/N	Y/N	Y/N	Y/N
5	toilet	Y/N	Y/N	Y/N	Y/N	Y/N
5g	generalization	Y/N	Y/N	Y/N	Y/N	Y/N
6	spoon	Y/N	Y/N	Y/N	Y/N	Y/N
6g	generalization	Y/N	Y/N	Y/N	Y/N	Y/N
7	plate	Y/N	Y/N	Y/N	Y/N	Y/N
7g	generalization	Y/N	Y/N	Y/N	Y/N	Y/N
8	book	Y/N	Y/N	Y/N	Y/N	Y/N
8g	generalization	Y/N	Y/N	Y/N	Y/N	Y/N
9	toy	Y/N	Y/N	Y/N	Y/N	Y/N

9g	generalization	Y/N	Y/N	Y/N	Y/N	Y/N
10	crayon	Y/N	Y/N	Y/N	Y/N	Y/N
10g	generalization	Y/N	Y/N	Y/N	Y/N	Y/N
11	paper	Y/N	Y/N	Y/N	Y/N	Y/N
11g	generalization	Y/N	Y/N	Y/N	Y/N	Y/N
12	computer	Y/N	Y/N	Y/N	Y/N	Y/N
12g	generalization	Y/N	Y/N	Y/N	Y/N	Y/N
13	window	Y/N	Y/N	Y/N	Y/N	Y/N
13g	generalization	Y/N	Y/N	Y/N	Y/N	Y/N
14	teddy bear	Y/N	Y/N	Y/N	Y/N	Y/N
14g	generalization	Y/N	Y/N	Y/N	Y/N	Y/N
15	candy	Y/N	Y/N	Y/N	Y/N	Y/N
15g	generalization	Y/N	Y/N	Y/N	Y/N	Y/N
16	camera	Y/N	Y/N	Y/N	Y/N	Y/N
16g	generalization	Y/N	Y/N	Y/N	Y/N	Y/N
17	phone	Y/N	Y/N	Y/N	Y/N	Y/N
17g	generalization	Y/N	Y/N	Y/N	Y/N	Y/N
18	sock	Y/N	Y/N	Y/N	Y/N	Y/N
18g	generalization	Y/N	Y/N	Y/N	Y/N	Y/N
19	shoe	Y/N	Y/N	Y/N	Y/N	Y/N
19g	generalization	Y/N	Y/N	Y/N	Y/N	Y/N

Child Name: . . . .

Expressive Identification of Objects

Teaching Procedure: Present the child with the direction "WHAT IS THIS? _____ [WHILE HOLDING UP OBJECT/POINTING TO OBJECT]."

Materials: Objects presented in the steps below.

	STEPS					
1	sock	Y/N	Y/N	Y/N	Y/N	Y/N
1g	generalization	Y/N	Y/N	Y/N	Y/N	Y/N
2	shoe	Y/N	Y/N	Y/N	Y/N	Y/N
2g	generalization	Y/N	Y/N	Y/N	Y/N	Y/N
3	pencil	Y/N	Y/N	Y/N	Y/N	Y/N
3g	generalization	Y/N	Y/N	Y/N	Y/N	Y/N
4	paper	Y/N	Y/N	Y/N	Y/N	Y/N
4g	generalization	Y/N	Y/N	Y/N	Y/N	Y/N
5	crayon	Y/N	Y/N	Y/N	Y/N	Y/N
5g	generalization	Y/N	Y/N	Y/N	Y/N	Y/N
6	cup	Y/N	Y/N	Y/N	Y/N	Y/N
6g	generalization	Y/N	Y/N	Y/N	Y/N	Y/N
7	camera	Y/N	Y/N	Y/N	Y/N	Y/N
7g	generalization	Y/N	Y/N	Y/N	Y/N	Y/N
8	phone	Y/N	Y/N	Y/N	Y/N	Y/N
8g	generalization	Y/N	Y/N	Y/N	Y/N	Y/N
9	television	Y/N	Y/N	Y/N	Y/N	Y/N

9g	generalization	Y/N	Y/N	Y/N	Y/N	Y/N
10	door	Y/N	Y/N	Y/N	Y/N	Y/N
10g	generalization	Y/N	Y/N	Y/N	Y/N	Y/N
11	toilet	Y/N	Y/N	Y/N	Y/N	Y/N
11g	generalization	Y/N	Y/N	Y/N	Y/N	Y/N
12	sink	Y/N	Y/N	Y/N	Y/N	Y/N
12g	generalization	Y/N	Y/N	Y/N	Y/N	Y/N
13	book	Y/N	Y/N	Y/N	Y/N	Y/N
13g	generalization	Y/N	Y/N	Y/N	Y/N	Y/N
14	balloons	Y/N	Y/N	Y/N	Y/N	Y/N
14g	generalization	Y/N	Y/N	Y/N	Y/N	Y/N
15	table	Y/N	Y/N	Y/N	Y/N	Y/N
15g	generalization	Y/N	Y/N	Y/N	Y/N	Y/N
16	chair	Y/N	Y/N	Y/N	Y/N	Y/N
16g	generalization	Y/N	Y/N	Y/N	Y/N	Y/N
17	teddy bear	Y/N	Y/N	Y/N	Y/N	Y/N
17g	generalization	Y/N	Y/N	Y/N	Y/N	Y/N
18	candy	Y/N	Y/N	Y/N	Y/N	Y/N
18g	generalization	Y/N	Y/N	Y/N	Y/N	Y/N
19	blocks	Y/N	Y/N	Y/N	Y/N	Y/N
19g	generalization	Y/N	Y/N	Y/N	Y/N	Y/N

Child Name: . . . .

Expressive Identification of Body Parts

Teaching Procedure: Present the child with the direction: POINT TO A BODY PART AND ASK CHILD TO NAME IT.

Materials: Dolls, pictures.

Note: Generalization of this program should be labeling body parts on other items: other people, dolls, pictures, etc.

	STEPS					
1	nose	Y/N	Y/N	Y/N	Y/N	Y/N
1g	generalization	Y/N	Y/N	Y/N	Y/N	Y/N
2	eyes	Y/N	Y/N	Y/N	Y/N	Y/N
2g	generalization	Y/N	Y/N	Y/N	Y/N	Y/N
3	ears	Y/N	Y/N	Y/N	Y/N	Y/N
3g	generalization	Y/N	Y/N	Y/N	Y/N	Y/N
4	mouth	Y/N	Y/N	Y/N	Y/N	Y/N
4g	generalization	Y/N	Y/N	Y/N	Y/N	Y/N
5	arm	Y/N	Y/N	Y/N	Y/N	Y/N
5g	generalization	Y/N	Y/N	Y/N	Y/N	Y/N
6	leg	Y/N	Y/N	Y/N	Y/N	Y/N
6g	generalization	Y/N	Y/N	Y/N	Y/N	Y/N
7	foot	Y/N	Y/N	Y/N	Y/N	Y/N
7g	generalization	Y/N	Y/N	Y/N	Y/N	Y/N
8	hand	Y/N	Y/N	Y/N	Y/N	Y/N

8g	generalization	Y/N	Y/N	Y/N	Y/N	Y/N
9	elbow	Y/N	Y/N	Y/N	Y/N	Y/N
9g	generalization	Y/N	Y/N	Y/N	Y/N	Y/N
10	knee	Y/N	Y/N	Y/N	Y/N	Y/N
10g	generalization	Y/N	Y/N	Y/N	Y/N	Y/N
11	chin	Y/N	Y/N	Y/N	Y/N	Y/N
11g	generalization	Y/N	Y/N	Y/N	Y/N	Y/N
12	head	Y/N	Y/N	Y/N	Y/N	Y/N
12g	generalization	Y/N	Y/N	Y/N	Y/N	Y/N
13	hair	Y/N	Y/N	Y/N	Y/N	Y/N
13g	generalization	Y/N	Y/N	Y/N	Y/N	Y/N
14	back	Y/N	Y/N	Y/N	Y/N	Y/N
14g	generalization	Y/N	Y/N	Y/N	Y/N	Y/N
15	stomach	Y/N	Y/N	Y/N	Y/N	Y/N
15g	generalization	Y/N	Y/N	Y/N	Y/N	Y/N
16	forehead	Y/N	Y/N	Y/N	Y/N	Y/N
16g	generalization	Y/N	Y/N	Y/N	Y/N	Y/N
17	neck	Y/N	Y/N	Y/N	Y/N	Y/N
17g	generalization	Y/N	Y/N	Y/N	Y/N	Y/N
18	tongue	Y/N	Y/N	Y/N	Y/N	Y/N
18g	generalization	Y/N	Y/N	Y/N	Y/N	Y/N

Child Name: . . . .

Expressive Identification of Articles of Clothing

Teaching Procedure: Hold up the article of clothing and ask the child "WHAT IS IT?" Generalization should include identifying the clothing on self and on others.

Materials: Various articles of clothing.

	STEPS					
1	shirt	Y/N	Y/N	Y/N	Y/N	Y/N
1g	generalization	Y/N	Y/N	Y/N	Y/N	Y/N
2	pants	Y/N	Y/N	Y/N	Y/N	Y/N
2g	generalization	Y/N	Y/N	Y/N	Y/N	Y/N
3	socks	Y/N	Y/N	Y/N	Y/N	Y/N
3g	generalization	Y/N	Y/N	Y/N	Y/N	Y/N
4	shoes	Y/N	Y/N	Y/N	Y/N	Y/N
4g	generalization	Y/N	Y/N	Y/N	Y/N	Y/N
5	underwear/diaper	Y/N	Y/N	Y/N	Y/N	Y/N
5g	generalization	Y/N	Y/N	Y/N	Y/N	Y/N
6	shorts	Y/N	Y/N	Y/N	Y/N	Y/N
6g	generalization	Y/N	Y/N	Y/N	Y/N	Y/N
7	jacket	Y/N	Y/N	Y/N	Y/N	Y/N
7g	generalization	Y/N	Y/N	Y/N	Y/N	Y/N
8	hat	Y/N	Y/N	Y/N	Y/N	Y/N
8g	generalization	Y/N	Y/N	Y/N	Y/N	Y/N
9	gloves	Y/N	Y/N	Y/N	Y/N	Y/N
9g	generalization	Y/N	Y/N	Y/N	Y/N	Y/N

Child Name:. . . . .

Expressive Identification of Familiar People

Teaching Procedure: Present the child with the direction "WHO IS THIS? _____ [WHILE HOLDING UP PICTURE]."

Materials: Pictures of people stated below.

Note: Generalization should be actual person and other pictures of the person, in addition to presenting the child with the picture in different settings and with different people.

	STEPS					
1	mom	Y/N	Y/N	Y/N	Y/N	Y/N
1g	generalization	Y/N	Y/N	Y/N	Y/N	Y/N
2	dad	Y/N	Y/N	Y/N	Y/N	Y/N
2g	generalization	Y/N	Y/N	Y/N	Y/N	Y/N
3	sibling	Y/N	Y/N	Y/N	Y/N	Y/N
3g	generalization	Y/N	Y/N	Y/N	Y/N	Y/N
4	grandmother	Y/N	Y/N	Y/N	Y/N	Y/N
4g	generalization	Y/N	Y/N	Y/N	Y/N	Y/N
5	teacher	Y/N	Y/N	Y/N	Y/N	Y/N
5g	generalization	Y/N	Y/N	Y/N	Y/N	Y/N
6	friend	Y/N	Y/N	Y/N	Y/N	Y/N
6g	generalization	Y/N	Y/N	Y/N	Y/N	Y/N

Child Name: . . . .

Expressive Identification of Emotions

Teaching Procedure: Direction: "HOW IS THE PERSON FEELING?"

Materials: Picture cards of the emotions. You can obtain picture cards of emotions through the websites www.do2learn.com and www.difflearn.com. You can also take pictures of yourself demonstrating different emotions.

Note: Generalization should be actual people acting out the emotion which can include television.

	STEPS					
1	happy	Y/N	Y/N	Y/N	Y/N	Y/N
1g	generalization	Y/N	Y/N	Y/N	Y/N	Y/N
2	sad	Y/N	Y/N	Y/N	Y/N	Y/N
2g	generalization	Y/N	Y/N	Y/N	Y/N	Y/N
3	angry/mad	Y/N	Y/N	Y/N	Y/N	Y/N
3g	generalization	Y/N	Y/N	Y/N	Y/N	Y/N
4	surprised	Y/N	Y/N	Y/N	Y/N	Y/N
4g	generalization	Y/N	Y/N	Y/N	Y/N	Y/N
5	scared	Y/N	Y/N	Y/N	Y/N	Y/N
5g	generalization	Y/N	Y/N	Y/N	Y/N	Y/N
6	bored	Y/N	Y/N	Y/N	Y/N	Y/N
6g	generalization	Y/N	Y/N	Y/N	Y/N	Y/N
7	embarrassed	Y/N	Y/N	Y/N	Y/N	Y/N
7g	generalization	Y/N	Y/N	Y/N	Y/N	Y/N

Child Name: . . . .

Expressive Identification of Community Helpers

Teaching Procedure: Present the child with the direction "WHO IS THIS PERSON? _____ [WHILE HOLDING UP PICTURE/POINTING TO PICTURE]."

Materials: Pictures presented in the steps below.

Note: Generalization should try to include the child identifying an actual community helper, and not just through pictures.

	STEPS					
1	policeman	Y/N	Y/N	Y/N	Y/N	Y/N
1g	generalization	Y/N	Y/N	Y/N	Y/N	Y/N
2	fireman	Y/N	Y/N	Y/N	Y/N	Y/N
2g	generalization	Y/N	Y/N	Y/N	Y/N	Y/N
3	mail man	Y/N	Y/N	Y/N	Y/N	Y/N
3g	generalization	Y/N	Y/N	Y/N	Y/N	Y/N
4	doctor	Y/N	Y/N	Y/N	Y/N	Y/N
4g	generalization	Y/N	Y/N	Y/N	Y/N	Y/N
5	nurse	Y/N	Y/N	Y/N	Y/N	Y/N
5g	generalization	Y/N	Y/N	Y/N	Y/N	Y/N
6	bus driver	Y/N	Y/N	Y/N	Y/N	Y/N
6g	generalization	Y/N	Y/N	Y/N	Y/N	Y/N
7	waiter	Y/N	Y/N	Y/N	Y/N	Y/N
7g	generalization	Y/N	Y/N	Y/N	Y/N	Y/N
8	teacher	Y/N	Y/N	Y/N	Y/N	Y/N
8g	generalization	Y/N	Y/N	Y/N	Y/N	Y/N

Child Name: . . . .

Expressive Identification of Environmental Sounds

Teaching Procedure: Present the child with the direction "WHAT SOUND DO YOU HEAR?"

Materials: Sounds of a dog barking, a fire truck siren, a train whistle, a horn, an airplane, an ambulance siren, a bird chirping, a telephone ringing, a door bell, a baby crying.

	STEPS					
1	dog	Y/N	Y/N	Y/N	Y/N	Y/N
1g	generalization	Y/N	Y/N	Y/N	Y/N	Y/N
2	fire truck	Y/N	Y/N	Y/N	Y/N	Y/N
2g	generalization	Y/N	Y/N	Y/N	Y/N	Y/N
3	train	Y/N	Y/N	Y/N	Y/N	Y/N
3g	generalization	Y/N	Y/N	Y/N	Y/N	Y/N
4	horn (on car)	Y/N	Y/N	Y/N	Y/N	Y/N
4g	generalization	Y/N	Y/N	Y/N	Y/N	Y/N
5	airplane	Y/N	Y/N	Y/N	Y/N	Y/N
5g	generalization	Y/N	Y/N	Y/N	Y/N	Y/N
6	ambulance	Y/N	Y/N	Y/N	Y/N	Y/N
6g	generalization	Y/N	Y/N	Y/N	Y/N	Y/N
7	bird	Y/N	Y/N	Y/N	Y/N	Y/N
7g	generalization	Y/N	Y/N	Y/N	Y/N	Y/N
8	telephone ringing	Y/N	Y/N	Y/N	Y/N	Y/N
8g	generalization	Y/N	Y/N	Y/N	Y/N	Y/N
9	door bell	Y/N	Y/N	Y/N	Y/N	Y/N
9g	generalization	Y/N	Y/N	Y/N	Y/N	Y/N
10	baby crying	Y/N	Y/N	Y/N	Y/N	Y/N
10g	generalization	Y/N	Y/N	Y/N	Y/N	Y/N

Action Programs

Child Name: . . . .

Receptive Identification of Actions

Teaching Procedure: Present the child with the direction "SHOW ME/POINT TO/TOUCH _____ [ACTION]."

Materials: Pictures of items below.

	STEPS					
1	jumping	Y/N	Y/N	Y/N	Y/N	Y/N
1g	generalization	Y/N	Y/N	Y/N	Y/N	Y/N
2	hopping	Y/N	Y/N	Y/N	Y/N	Y/N
2g	generalization	Y/N	Y/N	Y/N	Y/N	Y/N
3	walking	Y/N	Y/N	Y/N	Y/N	Y/N
3g	generalization	Y/N	Y/N	Y/N	Y/N	Y/N
4	sleeping	Y/N	Y/N	Y/N	Y/N	Y/N
4g	generalization	Y/N	Y/N	Y/N	Y/N	Y/N
5	hugging	Y/N	Y/N	Y/N	Y/N	Y/N
5g	generalization	Y/N	Y/N	Y/N	Y/N	Y/N
6	sitting	Y/N	Y/N	Y/N	Y/N	Y/N
6g	generalization	Y/N	Y/N	Y/N	Y/N	Y/N
7	drinking	Y/N	Y/N	Y/N	Y/N	Y/N
7g	generalization	Y/N	Y/N	Y/N	Y/N	Y/N
8	eating	Y/N	Y/N	Y/N	Y/N	Y/N
8g	generalization	Y/N	Y/N	Y/N	Y/N	Y/N

9	falling	Y/N	Y/N	Y/N	Y/N	Y/N
9g	generalization	Y/N	Y/N	Y/N	Y/N	Y/N
10	playing	Y/N	Y/N	Y/N	Y/N	Y/N
10g	generalization	Y/N	Y/N	Y/N	Y/N	Y/N
11	cutting	Y/N	Y/N	Y/N	Y/N	Y/N
11g	generalization	Y/N	Y/N	Y/N	Y/N	Y/N
12	crying	Y/N	Y/N	Y/N	Y/N	Y/N
12g	generalization	Y/N	Y/N	Y/N	Y/N	Y/N
13	brushing	Y/N	Y/N	Y/N	Y/N	Y/N
13g	generalization	Y/N	Y/N	Y/N	Y/N	Y/N
14	blowing	Y/N	Y/N	Y/N	Y/N	Y/N
14g	generalization	Y/N	Y/N	Y/N	Y/N	Y/N
15	dancing	Y/N	Y/N	Y/N	Y/N	Y/N
15g	generalization	Y/N	Y/N	Y/N	Y/N	Y/N
16	crawling	Y/N	Y/N	Y/N	Y/N	Y/N
16g	generalization	Y/N	Y/N	Y/N	Y/N	Y/N
17	reading	Y/N	Y/N	Y/N	Y/N	Y/N
17g	generalization	Y/N	Y/N	Y/N	Y/N	Y/N
18	drawing	Y/N	Y/N	Y/N	Y/N	Y/N
18g	generalization	Y/N	Y/N	Y/N	Y/N	Y/N

Child Name: . . . .

Expressive Identification of Actions

Teaching Procedure: Present the child with the direction "WHAT IS THE PERSON DOING? _____ [WHILE HOLDING UP PICTURE/POINTING TO PICTURE]."

Materials: Pictures presented in the steps below.

Note: Generalization should include an actual person acting out the action with the direction "What am I doing?"

	STEPS					
1	jumping	Y/N	Y/N	Y/N	Y/N	Y/N
1g	generalization	Y/N	Y/N	Y/N	Y/N	Y/N
2	hopping	Y/N	Y/N	Y/N	Y/N	Y/N
2g	generalization	Y/N	Y/N	Y/N	Y/N	Y/N
3	walking	Y/N	Y/N	Y/N	Y/N	Y/N
3g	generalization	Y/N	Y/N	Y/N	Y/N	Y/N
4	sleeping	Y/N	Y/N	Y/N	Y/N	Y/N
4g	generalization	Y/N	Y/N	Y/N	Y/N	Y/N
5	hugging	Y/N	Y/N	Y/N	Y/N	Y/N
5g	generalization	Y/N	Y/N	Y/N	Y/N	Y/N
6	sitting	Y/N	Y/N	Y/N	Y/N	Y/N
6g	generalization	Y/N	Y/N	Y/N	Y/N	Y/N
7	drinking	Y/N	Y/N	Y/N	Y/N	Y/N
7g	generalization	Y/N	Y/N	Y/N	Y/N	Y/N
8	eating	Y/N	Y/N	Y/N	Y/N	Y/N

8g	generalization	Y/N	Y/N	Y/N	Y/N	Y/N
9	falling	Y/N	Y/N	Y/N	Y/N	Y/N
9g	generalization	Y/N	Y/N	Y/N	Y/N	Y/N
10	playing	Y/N	Y/N	Y/N	Y/N	Y/N
10g	generalization	Y/N	Y/N	Y/N	Y/N	Y/N
11	cutting	Y/N	Y/N	Y/N	Y/N	Y/N
11g	generalization	Y/N	Y/N	Y/N	Y/N	Y/N
12	crying	Y/N	Y/N	Y/N	Y/N	Y/N
12g	generalization	Y/N	Y/N	Y/N	Y/N	Y/N
13	brushing	Y/N	Y/N	Y/N	Y/N	Y/N
13g	generalization	Y/N	Y/N	Y/N	Y/N	Y/N
14	blowing	Y/N	Y/N	Y/N	Y/N	Y/N
14g	generalization	Y/N	Y/N	Y/N	Y/N	Y/N
15	dancing	Y/N	Y/N	Y/N	Y/N	Y/N
15g	generalization	Y/N	Y/N	Y/N	Y/N	Y/N
16	crawling	Y/N	Y/N	Y/N	Y/N	Y/N
16g	generalization	Y/N	Y/N	Y/N	Y/N	Y/N
17	reading	Y/N	Y/N	Y/N	Y/N	Y/N
17g	generalization	Y/N	Y/N	Y/N	Y/N	Y/N
18	drawing	Y/N	Y/N	Y/N	Y/N	Y/N
18g	generalization	Y/N	Y/N	Y/N	Y/N	Y/N

Child Name: . . . .

Imitates Actions of Others

Teaching Procedure: Start to do the action while making sure the child is attending. Do not ask the child to do what you are doing, or to look at you. The purpose of this program is for the child to start to naturally pick up on what you/others are doing and just imitate them.

Materials: None.

	STEPS					
1	clap hands	Y/N	Y/N	Y/N	Y/N	Y/N
1g	generalization	Y/N	Y/N	Y/N	Y/N	Y/N
2	stamp feet	Y/N	Y/N	Y/N	Y/N	Y/N
2g	generalization	Y/N	Y/N	Y/N	Y/N	Y/N
3	jump	Y/N	Y/N	Y/N	Y/N	Y/N
3g	generalization	Y/N	Y/N	Y/N	Y/N	Y/N
4	sit down	Y/N	Y/N	Y/N	Y/N	Y/N
4g	generalization	Y/N	Y/N	Y/N	Y/N	Y/N
5	stand up	Y/N	Y/N	Y/N	Y/N	Y/N
5g	generalization	Y/N	Y/N	Y/N	Y/N	Y/N

Child Name: . . . .

Imitates Two Step Actions

Teaching Procedure: Present the child with the direction "DO THIS __."
Materials: None.

	STEPS					
1	clap hands, tap thighs (after model has finished)	Y/N	Y/N	Y/N	Y/N	Y/N
1g	generalization	Y/N	Y/N	Y/N	Y/N	Y/N
2	stand up, turn around (after model has finished)	Y/N	Y/N	Y/N	Y/N	Y/N
2g	generalization	Y/N	Y/N	Y/N	Y/N	Y/N
3	tap table, wave (after model has finished)	Y/N	Y/N	Y/N	Y/N	Y/N
3g	generalization	Y/N	Y/N	Y/N	Y/N	Y/N
4	arms up, arms on hips (after model has finished)	Y/N	Y/N	Y/N	Y/N	Y/N
4g	generalization	Y/N	Y/N	Y/N	Y/N	Y/N
5	touch head, hands on shoulders (after model has finished)	Y/N	Y/N	Y/N	Y/N	Y/N
5g	generalization	Y/N	Y/N	Y/N	Y/N	Y/N
6	stamp feet, clap hands (after model has finished)	Y/N	Y/N	Y/N	Y/N	Y/N
6g	generalization	Y/N	Y/N	Y/N	Y/N	Y/N
7	feet together, feet apart (after model has finished)	Y/N	Y/N	Y/N	Y/N	Y/N
7g	generalization	Y/N	Y/N	Y/N	Y/N	Y/N
8	rub tummy, open mouth (after model has finished)	Y/N	Y/N	Y/N	Y/N	Y/N
8g	generalization	Y/N	Y/N	Y/N	Y/N	Y/N
9	open and close mouth, wave (after model has finished)	Y/N	Y/N	Y/N	Y/N	Y/N
9g	generalization	Y/N	Y/N	Y/N	Y/N	Y/N
10	jump, sit down (after model has finished)	Y/N	Y/N	Y/N	Y/N	Y/N
10g	generalization	Y/N	Y/N	Y/N	Y/N	Y/N

Child Name: . . . .

Pretends to do an Action

Teaching Procedure: Present the child with the direction "SHOW ME HOW YOU _____ [NAME ACTION]."

Materials: Dolls, pictures, actual articles of clothing.

Note: This program differs from expressive action identification in that the child is the one acting out the action.

	STEPS					
1	laughing	Y/N	Y/N	Y/N	Y/N	Y/N
1g	generalization	Y/N	Y/N	Y/N	Y/N	Y/N
2	crying	Y/N	Y/N	Y/N	Y/N	Y/N
2g	generalization	Y/N	Y/N	Y/N	Y/N	Y/N
3	sleeping	Y/N	Y/N	Y/N	Y/N	Y/N
3g	generalization	Y/N	Y/N	Y/N	Y/N	Y/N
4	writing	Y/N	Y/N	Y/N	Y/N	Y/N
4g	generalization	Y/N	Y/N	Y/N	Y/N	Y/N
5	cutting	Y/N	Y/N	Y/N	Y/N	Y/N
5g	generalization	Y/N	Y/N	Y/N	Y/N	Y/N
6	jumping	Y/N	Y/N	Y/N	Y/N	Y/N
6g	generalization	Y/N	Y/N	Y/N	Y/N	Y/N
7	dancing	Y/N	Y/N	Y/N	Y/N	Y/N
7g	generalization	Y/N	Y/N	Y/N	Y/N	Y/N
8	reading	Y/N	Y/N	Y/N	Y/N	Y/N
8g	generalization	Y/N	Y/N	Y/N	Y/N	Y/N
9	eating	Y/N	Y/N	Y/N	Y/N	Y/N
9g	generalization	Y/N	Y/N	Y/N	Y/N	Y/N
10	drinking	Y/N	Y/N	Y/N	Y/N	Y/N
10g	generalization	Y/N	Y/N	Y/N	Y/N	Y/N

Communication Programs

Child Name: . . . .

Points to Communicate

Teaching Procedure: Present the child with the direction "SHOW ME WHAT YOU WANT."

Materials: Preferred objects that the child would want.

	STEPS					
1	hold up reinforcing object and present direction	Y/N	Y/N	Y/N	Y/N	Y/N
1g	generalization	Y/N	Y/N	Y/N	Y/N	Y/N
2	hold up 2 reinforcing objects and present direction	Y/N	Y/N	Y/N	Y/N	Y/N
2g	generalization	Y/N	Y/N	Y/N	Y/N	Y/N
3	child will point to desired object in a field of 3 when presented with direction	Y/N	Y/N	Y/N	Y/N	Y/N
3g	generalization	Y/N	Y/N	Y/N	Y/N	Y/N
4	child will point to any known item when asked to find it	Y/N	Y/N	Y/N	Y/N	Y/N
4g	generalization	Y/N	Y/N	Y/N	Y/N	Y/N
5	child will show you what they want by pointing to it	Y/N	Y/N	Y/N	Y/N	Y/N
5g	generalization	Y/N	Y/N	Y/N	Y/N	Y/N

Child Name:. . . . .

Yes/No

Teaching Procedure: Present the child with the direction "DO YOU WANT THIS ___?"

Materials: Preferred and non-preferred items.

Note: To identify a preferred item, allow the child to get up and play with what he or she wants. After 2–3 seconds of play, take item away and present the direction "Do you want this?" To make sure there is no confusion for non-preferred items, use something that is not a toy or a potential reinforcer.

	STEPS					
1	present the child with a preferred item and present direction	Y/N	Y/N	Y/N	Y/N	Y/N
1g	generalization	Y/N	Y/N	Y/N	Y/N	Y/N
2	present the child with a non-preferred item and present direction	Y/N	Y/N	Y/N	Y/N	Y/N
2g	generalization	Y/N	Y/N	Y/N	Y/N	Y/N
3	randomly present preferred and non-preferred items	Y/N	Y/N	Y/N	Y/N	Y/N
3g	generalization	Y/N	Y/N	Y/N	Y/N	Y/N

Child Name: . . . .

Manding

Teaching Procedure: Present the child with situations in which they would need to mand for the item/object/etc. (see steps below). If you provide them with the visual it is considered a prompted mand.

Materials: None.

Note: A mand is when the child communicates their wants and needs to another person without being asked "What do you want?" It can be in the form of a gesture, sign language, picture exchange, or words. The point of manding is to get the child to be able to walk up to another person and be able to "mand" for the item that they want. You can think of a mand as the child demanding or requesting an item.

	STEPS					
1	open	Y/N	Y/N	Y/N	Y/N	Y/N
1g	generalization	Y/N	Y/N	Y/N	Y/N	Y/N
2	eat	Y/N	Y/N	Y/N	Y/N	Y/N
2g	generalization	Y/N	Y/N	Y/N	Y/N	Y/N
3	drink	Y/N	Y/N	Y/N	Y/N	Y/N
3g	generalization	Y/N	Y/N	Y/N	Y/N	Y/N
4	help me	Y/N	Y/N	Y/N	Y/N	Y/N
4g	generalization	Y/N	Y/N	Y/N	Y/N	Y/N
5	sit down	Y/N	Y/N	Y/N	Y/N	Y/N
5g	generalization	Y/N	Y/N	Y/N	Y/N	Y/N
6	stand up	Y/N	Y/N	Y/N	Y/N	Y/N
6g	generalization	Y/N	Y/N	Y/N	Y/N	Y/N
7	play	Y/N	Y/N	Y/N	Y/N	Y/N
7g	generalization	Y/N	Y/N	Y/N	Y/N	Y/N
8	close	Y/N	Y/N	Y/N	Y/N	Y/N
8g	generalization	Y/N	Y/N	Y/N	Y/N	Y/N
9	all done	Y/N	Y/N	Y/N	Y/N	Y/N
9g	generalization	Y/N	Y/N	Y/N	Y/N	Y/N

Child Name: . . . .

Requests with Eye Contact

Teaching Procedure: Wait for the child to look at you before responding to their request. If the child does not look at you within 5 seconds of the request, prompt them.

Materials: None.

Note: A request can be in the form of a gesture, sign language, picture exchange, or words.

	STEPS					
1	looks at person for a couple of seconds at some point during the request	Y/N	Y/N	Y/N	Y/N	Y/N
1g	generalization	Y/N	Y/N	Y/N	Y/N	Y/N
2	looks at person at the start of the request	Y/N	Y/N	Y/N	Y/N	Y/N
2g	generalization	Y/N	Y/N	Y/N	Y/N	Y/N
3	looks at person at the start of the request and at the end of the request	Y/N	Y/N	Y/N	Y/N	Y/N
3g	generalization	Y/N	Y/N	Y/N	Y/N	Y/N
4	looks at person for the entire request	Y/N	Y/N	Y/N	Y/N	Y/N
4g	generalization	Y/N	Y/N	Y/N	Y/N	Y/N

Child Name: . . . .

Gets Attention of Others

Teaching Procedure: Contrive a situation in which 1 person is busy. Tell the child to "GIVE ____ [THE BUSY PERSON] THE PIECE OF PAPER." Have the child walk over to the busy person and get their attention by either tapping their shoulder or calling their name.

Materials: None.

Note: Generalization should include using other directions than "give the paper to ____."

	STEPS					
1	will tap a person's shoulder to gain attention	Y/N	Y/N	Y/N	Y/N	Y/N
1g	generalization	Y/N	Y/N	Y/N	Y/N	Y/N
2	will call a person's name to gain attention	Y/N	Y/N	Y/N	Y/N	Y/N
2g	generalization	Y/N	Y/N	Y/N	Y/N	Y/N

Child Name: . . . .

Says Bye

Teaching Procedure: Direction: A PERSON LEAVING.

Materials: None.

	STEPS					
1	returns greeting	Y/N	Y/N	Y/N	Y/N	Y/N
1g	generalization	Y/N	Y/N	Y/N	Y/N	Y/N
2	initiates the goodbye when a person says "I am leaving"	Y/N	Y/N	Y/N	Y/N	Y/N
2g	generalization	Y/N	Y/N	Y/N	Y/N	Y/N

Child Name:. . . . .

Says Hi

Teaching Procedure: Direction: THE ARRIVAL OF A PERSON.
Materials: None.

	STEPS					
1	says "Hi" to person first	Y/N	Y/N	Y/N	Y/N	Y/N
1g	generalization	Y/N	Y/N	Y/N	Y/N	Y/N
2	responds with "Hi" when the person says "Hi" first	Y/N	Y/N	Y/N	Y/N	Y/N
2g	generalization	Y/N	Y/N	Y/N	Y/N	Y/N

Child Name:. . . . .

Imitates Sounds

Teaching Procedure: Present the child with the direction: "SAY _____."
Materials: None.

	STEPS					
1	/a/	Y/N	Y/N	Y/N	Y/N	Y/N
1g	generalization	Y/N	Y/N	Y/N	Y/N	Y/N
2	/m/	Y/N	Y/N	Y/N	Y/N	Y/N
2g	generalization	Y/N	Y/N	Y/N	Y/N	Y/N
3	/d/	Y/N	Y/N	Y/N	Y/N	Y/N
3g	generalization	Y/N	Y/N	Y/N	Y/N	Y/N
4	/h/	Y/N	Y/N	Y/N	Y/N	Y/N
4g	generalization	Y/N	Y/N	Y/N	Y/N	Y/N
5	/p/	Y/N	Y/N	Y/N	Y/N	Y/N
5g	generalization	Y/N	Y/N	Y/N	Y/N	Y/N
6	/b/	Y/N	Y/N	Y/N	Y/N	Y/N
6g	generalization	Y/N	Y/N	Y/N	Y/N	Y/N
7	/t/	Y/N	Y/N	Y/N	Y/N	Y/N
7g	generalization	Y/N	Y/N	Y/N	Y/N	Y/N
8	/g/	Y/N	Y/N	Y/N	Y/N	Y/N
8g	generalization	Y/N	Y/N	Y/N	Y/N	Y/N
9	/n/	Y/N	Y/N	Y/N	Y/N	Y/N
9g	generalization	Y/N	Y/N	Y/N	Y/N	Y/N

Child Name: . . . .

Uses Different Words to Request

Teaching Procedure: This program should be taught with reinforcing items. Present the reinforcing item and follow the steps below. The direction is the presence of the reinforcing item.

Materials: Highly motivating items that the child will want to request.

	STEPS					
1	I want	Y/N	Y/N	Y/N	Y/N	Y/N
1g	generalization	Y/N	Y/N	Y/N	Y/N	Y/N
2	Can I have	Y/N	Y/N	Y/N	Y/N	Y/N
2g	generalization	Y/N	Y/N	Y/N	Y/N	Y/N
3	Give me please	Y/N	Y/N	Y/N	Y/N	Y/N
3g	generalization	Y/N	Y/N	Y/N	Y/N	Y/N
4	I need	Y/N	Y/N	Y/N	Y/N	Y/N
4g	generalization	Y/N	Y/N	Y/N	Y/N	Y/N

Intraverbal Programs

Child Name: . . . .

Common Animal Intraverbals

Teaching Procedure: Present the child with the direction: "A _____ [FILL IN ANIMAL] SAYS _____."
Materials: None.

	STEPS					
1	dog (woof or bark)	Y/N	Y/N	Y/N	Y/N	Y/N
1g	generalization	Y/N	Y/N	Y/N	Y/N	Y/N
2	cat (meow)	Y/N	Y/N	Y/N	Y/N	Y/N
2g	generalization	Y/N	Y/N	Y/N	Y/N	Y/N
3	cow (moo)	Y/N	Y/N	Y/N	Y/N	Y/N
3g	generalization	Y/N	Y/N	Y/N	Y/N	Y/N
4	pig (oink)	Y/N	Y/N	Y/N	Y/N	Y/N
4g	generalization	Y/N	Y/N	Y/N	Y/N	Y/N
5	horse (neigh)	Y/N	Y/N	Y/N	Y/N	Y/N
5g	generalization	Y/N	Y/N	Y/N	Y/N	Y/N
6	lion (roar)	Y/N	Y/N	Y/N	Y/N	Y/N
6g	generalization	Y/N	Y/N	Y/N	Y/N	Y/N
7	bear (grrrr)	Y/N	Y/N	Y/N	Y/N	Y/N
7g	generalization	Y/N	Y/N	Y/N	Y/N	Y/N
8	monkey (ooo ooo ah ah)	Y/N	Y/N	Y/N	Y/N	Y/N
8g	generalization	Y/N	Y/N	Y/N	Y/N	Y/N
9	bird (chirp)	Y/N	Y/N	Y/N	Y/N	Y/N
9g	generalization	Y/N	Y/N	Y/N	Y/N	Y/N

Child Name: . . . .

Common Intraverbals

Teaching Procedure: Present the child with the first part of the fill-in and wait for the child to respond. For example in step 1: up and ___ (wait for child to say "down").

Materials: None.

	STEPS					
1	up and ___ (down)	Y/N	Y/N	Y/N	Y/N	Y/N
1g	generalization	Y/N	Y/N	Y/N	Y/N	Y/N
2	ready, set, ___ (go)	Y/N	Y/N	Y/N	Y/N	Y/N
2g	generalization	Y/N	Y/N	Y/N	Y/N	Y/N
3	1, 2, ___ (3)	Y/N	Y/N	Y/N	Y/N	Y/N
3g	generalization	Y/N	Y/N	Y/N	Y/N	Y/N
4	Winnie the ___ (Pooh)	Y/N	Y/N	Y/N	Y/N	Y/N
4g	generalization	Y/N	Y/N	Y/N	Y/N	Y/N
5	follow the ___ (leader)	Y/N	Y/N	Y/N	Y/N	Y/N
5g	generalization	Y/N	Y/N	Y/N	Y/N	Y/N
6	peek a ___ (boo)	Y/N	Y/N	Y/N	Y/N	Y/N
6g	generalization	Y/N	Y/N	Y/N	Y/N	Y/N
7	hide and ___ (seek)	Y/N	Y/N	Y/N	Y/N	Y/N
7g	generalization	Y/N	Y/N	Y/N	Y/N	Y/N
8	let's go ___ (play)	Y/N	Y/N	Y/N	Y/N	Y/N
8g	generalization	Y/N	Y/N	Y/N	Y/N	Y/N
9	go down the ___ (slide)	Y/N	Y/N	Y/N	Y/N	Y/N
9g	generalization	Y/N	Y/N	Y/N	Y/N	Y/N

Child Name: . . . .

Daily Activity Intraverbals

Teaching Procedure: Present the child with the question in each step. For example in step 1: "You wash your ___."

Materials: None.

	STEPS					
1	wash your ___ (hands)	Y/N	Y/N	Y/N	Y/N	Y/N
1g	generalization	Y/N	Y/N	Y/N	Y/N	Y/N
2	zip your ___ (jacket/coat)	Y/N	Y/N	Y/N	Y/N	Y/N
2g	generalization	Y/N	Y/N	Y/N	Y/N	Y/N
3	put on your ___ (shoes)	Y/N	Y/N	Y/N	Y/N	Y/N
3g	generalization	Y/N	Y/N	Y/N	Y/N	Y/N
4	brush your ___ (hair)	Y/N	Y/N	Y/N	Y/N	Y/N
4g	generalization	Y/N	Y/N	Y/N	Y/N	Y/N
5	sleep in a ___ (bed)	Y/N	Y/N	Y/N	Y/N	Y/N
5g	generalization	Y/N	Y/N	Y/N	Y/N	Y/N
6	you eat ___ (food)	Y/N	Y/N	Y/N	Y/N	Y/N
6g	generalization	Y/N	Y/N	Y/N	Y/N	Y/N
7	read the ___ (book)	Y/N	Y/N	Y/N	Y/N	Y/N
7g	generalization	Y/N	Y/N	Y/N	Y/N	Y/N
8	play with the ___ (toys)	Y/N	Y/N	Y/N	Y/N	Y/N
8g	generalization	Y/N	Y/N	Y/N	Y/N	Y/N
9	talk on the ___ (phone)	Y/N	Y/N	Y/N	Y/N	Y/N
9g	generalization	Y/N	Y/N	Y/N	Y/N	Y/N

Child Name: . . . .

Social Questions

Teaching Procedure: Present the child with the direction: ASK THE CHILD THE QUESTION IN EACH STEP. For example in step 1: "What is your name?"

Materials: None.

	STEPS					
1	name	Y/N	Y/N	Y/N	Y/N	Y/N
1g	generalization	Y/N	Y/N	Y/N	Y/N	Y/N
2	age	Y/N	Y/N	Y/N	Y/N	Y/N
2g	generalization	Y/N	Y/N	Y/N	Y/N	Y/N
3	name(s) of sibling(s)	Y/N	Y/N	Y/N	Y/N	Y/N
3g	generalization	Y/N	Y/N	Y/N	Y/N	Y/N
4	mom's name	Y/N	Y/N	Y/N	Y/N	Y/N
4g	generalization	Y/N	Y/N	Y/N	Y/N	Y/N
5	address	Y/N	Y/N	Y/N	Y/N	Y/N
5g	generalization	Y/N	Y/N	Y/N	Y/N	Y/N
6	city/town you live in	Y/N	Y/N	Y/N	Y/N	Y/N
6g	generalization	Y/N	Y/N	Y/N	Y/N	Y/N
7	state you live in	Y/N	Y/N	Y/N	Y/N	Y/N
7g	generalization	Y/N	Y/N	Y/N	Y/N	Y/N
8	telephone number	Y/N	Y/N	Y/N	Y/N	Y/N
8g	generalization	Y/N	Y/N	Y/N	Y/N	Y/N

Play Programs

Single Piece Puzzle

Teaching Procedure: Present the child with the direction "DO PUZZLE."

Materials: Single piece puzzles.

Note: Use a backward chaining procedure.

	STEPS					
1	instructor completes all puzzle pieces EXCEPT the last 1	Y/N	Y/N	Y/N	Y/N	Y/N
1g	generalization	Y/N	Y/N	Y/N	Y/N	Y/N
2	instructor completes all puzzle pieces EXCEPT the last 2	Y/N	Y/N	Y/N	Y/N	Y/N
2g	generalization	Y/N	Y/N	Y/N	Y/N	Y/N
3	instructor completes all puzzle pieces EXCEPT the last 3	Y/N	Y/N	Y/N	Y/N	Y/N
3g	generalization	Y/N	Y/N	Y/N	Y/N	Y/N
4	instructor completes all puzzle pieces EXCEPT the last 4	Y/N	Y/N	Y/N	Y/N	Y/N
4g	generalization	Y/N	Y/N	Y/N	Y/N	Y/N

Shape Sorter

Teaching Procedure: Present the child with the direction "PLAY WITH SHAPE SORTER" and follow the steps below.

Materials: Shape sorter.

	STEPS					
1	the child will place the circle in (or whatever shape you choose)	Y/N	Y/N	Y/N	Y/N	Y/N
1g	generalization (circle)	Y/N	Y/N	Y/N	Y/N	Y/N
2	the child will place the oval in (or whatever shape you choose)	Y/N	Y/N	Y/N	Y/N	Y/N
2g	generalization (both circle and oval)	Y/N	Y/N	Y/N	Y/N	Y/N
3	the child will place the square in (or whatever shape you choose)	Y/N	Y/N	Y/N	Y/N	Y/N
3g	generalization (circle, oval, and square)	Y/N	Y/N	Y/N	Y/N	Y/N
4	the child will place the triangle in (or whatever shape you choose)	Y/N	Y/N	Y/N	Y/N	Y/N
4g	generalization (circle, oval, square, and triangle)	Y/N	Y/N	Y/N	Y/N	Y/N
5	the child will place the rectangle in (or whatever shape you choose)	Y/N	Y/N	Y/N	Y/N	Y/N
5g	generalization (circle, oval, square, triangle, and rectangle)	Y/N	Y/N	Y/N	Y/N	Y/N
6	the child will place the star in (or whatever shape you choose)	Y/N	Y/N	Y/N	Y/N	Y/N
6g	generalization (circle, oval, square, triangle, rectangle, and star)	Y/N	Y/N	Y/N	Y/N	Y/N

Child Name:. . . . .

Plays By Self

Teaching Procedure: Present the child with the direction: "GO PLAY."

Materials: Toys the child is able to play with by themselves.

	STEPS					
1	30 seconds	Y/N	Y/N	Y/N	Y/N	Y/N
1g	generalization	Y/N	Y/N	Y/N	Y/N	Y/N
2	1 minute	Y/N	Y/N	Y/N	Y/N	Y/N
2g	generalization	Y/N	Y/N	Y/N	Y/N	Y/N
3	3 minutes	Y/N	Y/N	Y/N	Y/N	Y/N
3g	generalization	Y/N	Y/N	Y/N	Y/N	Y/N
4	5 minutes	Y/N	Y/N	Y/N	Y/N	Y/N
4g	generalization	Y/N	Y/N	Y/N	Y/N	Y/N
5	up to 10 minutes	Y/N	Y/N	Y/N	Y/N	Y/N
5g	generalization	Y/N	Y/N	Y/N	Y/N	Y/N

Child Name: ....

Various Methods of Play

Teaching Procedure: Present the child with the direction: STATE ACTION IN EACH STEP [E.G. BOUNCE BALL].

Materials: Various balls, various cars, brush, doll, cup, spoon, baby doll, car ramp, car tunnel, dog.

Note: Generalization should involve changing the direction to "play with [object]" and having the child demonstrate mastery of various methods of play.

	STEPS					
1	bounce ball	Y/N	Y/N	Y/N	Y/N	Y/N
1g	generalization	Y/N	Y/N	Y/N	Y/N	Y/N
2	roll ball	Y/N	Y/N	Y/N	Y/N	Y/N
2g	generalization	Y/N	Y/N	Y/N	Y/N	Y/N
3	throw ball	Y/N	Y/N	Y/N	Y/N	Y/N
3g	generalization	Y/N	Y/N	Y/N	Y/N	Y/N
4	kick ball	Y/N	Y/N	Y/N	Y/N	Y/N
4g	generalization	Y/N	Y/N	Y/N	Y/N	Y/N
5	make car go in a circle	Y/N	Y/N	Y/N	Y/N	Y/N
5g	generalization	Y/N	Y/N	Y/N	Y/N	Y/N
6	push car down ramp	Y/N	Y/N	Y/N	Y/N	Y/N
6g	generalization	Y/N	Y/N	Y/N	Y/N	Y/N
7	make car go through tunnel	Y/N	Y/N	Y/N	Y/N	Y/N
7g	generalization	Y/N	Y/N	Y/N	Y/N	Y/N
8	brush own hair	Y/N	Y/N	Y/N	Y/N	Y/N
8g	generalization	Y/N	Y/N	Y/N	Y/N	Y/N
9	brush doll hair	Y/N	Y/N	Y/N	Y/N	Y/N
9g	generalization	Y/N	Y/N	Y/N	Y/N	Y/N
10	brush teacher/parent hair	Y/N	Y/N	Y/N	Y/N	Y/N
10g	generalization	Y/N	Y/N	Y/N	Y/N	Y/N
11	drink from a cup	Y/N	Y/N	Y/N	Y/N	Y/N
11g	generalization	Y/N	Y/N	Y/N	Y/N	Y/N
12	pour water into a cup	Y/N	Y/N	Y/N	Y/N	Y/N
12g	generalization	Y/N	Y/N	Y/N	Y/N	Y/N
13	stir spoon in cup	Y/N	Y/N	Y/N	Y/N	Y/N
13g	generalization	Y/N	Y/N	Y/N	Y/N	Y/N
14	give baby a drink from the cup	Y/N	Y/N	Y/N	Y/N	Y/N
14g	generalization	Y/N	Y/N	Y/N	Y/N	Y/N

Child Name:..

Ball Play

Teaching Procedure: Present the child with the direction "LET'S PLAY WITH THE BALL [THEN STATE ACTION YOU WANT THE CHILD TO PERFORM]." Example (step 1): "let's play with the ball, let's roll it back and forth."

Materials: Ball.

	STEPS					
1	roll a ball back and forth	Y/N	Y/N	Y/N	Y/N	Y/N
1g	generalization	Y/N	Y/N	Y/N	Y/N	Y/N
2	roll the ball and knock down pins	Y/N	Y/N	Y/N	Y/N	Y/N
2g	generalization	Y/N	Y/N	Y/N	Y/N	Y/N
3	kick a ball back and forth	Y/N	Y/N	Y/N	Y/N	Y/N
3g	generalization	Y/N	Y/N	Y/N	Y/N	Y/N
4	kick a ball into a goal	Y/N	Y/N	Y/N	Y/N	Y/N
4g	generalization	Y/N	Y/N	Y/N	Y/N	Y/N
5	throw a ball back and forth	Y/N	Y/N	Y/N	Y/N	Y/N
5g	generalization	Y/N	Y/N	Y/N	Y/N	Y/N
6	throw a ball at a target	Y/N	Y/N	Y/N	Y/N	Y/N
6g	generalization	Y/N	Y/N	Y/N	Y/N	Y/N

Child Name: . . . .

Plays with Indoor Toys

Teaching Procedure: Present the child with the direction "PLAY WITH ___ [TOY]."

Materials: Shape sorter, pop-up toy, puzzle, doll/action hero.

Note: Suggested toys are provided; however, use toys that are in the child's home.

	STEPS					
1	shape sorter	Y/N	Y/N	Y/N	Y/N	Y/N
1g	generalization	Y/N	Y/N	Y/N	Y/N	Y/N
2	pop-up toy	Y/N	Y/N	Y/N	Y/N	Y/N
2g	generalization	Y/N	Y/N	Y/N	Y/N	Y/N
3	puzzle	Y/N	Y/N	Y/N	Y/N	Y/N
3g	generalization	Y/N	Y/N	Y/N	Y/N	Y/N
4	doll/action hero	Y/N	Y/N	Y/N	Y/N	Y/N
4g	generalization	Y/N	Y/N	Y/N	Y/N	Y/N
5	cars	Y/N	Y/N	Y/N	Y/N	Y/N
5g	generalization	Y/N	Y/N	Y/N	Y/N	Y/N

Child Name: . . . .

Outdoor Play

Teaching Procedure: Present the child with the direction "PLAY WITH/ON _____."
Materials: Slide, swing, chalk, ball.

	STEPS					
1	goes on slide	Y/N	Y/N	Y/N	Y/N	Y/N
1g	generalization	Y/N	Y/N	Y/N	Y/N	Y/N
2	goes on swing	Y/N	Y/N	Y/N	Y/N	Y/N
2g	generalization	Y/N	Y/N	Y/N	Y/N	Y/N
3	plays with chalk	Y/N	Y/N	Y/N	Y/N	Y/N
3g	generalization	Y/N	Y/N	Y/N	Y/N	Y/N
4	plays with a ball	Y/N	Y/N	Y/N	Y/N	Y/N
4g	generalization	Y/N	Y/N	Y/N	Y/N	Y/N

Child Name: . . . .

Uses Language While Playing

Teaching Procedure: Present the child with the direction "PLAY."

Materials: Toys that the child is able to play with independently.

Note: Try to use toys like a car so the child can say "vroom"; or for a train, "choo choo."

	STEPS					
1	uses at least 1 word for 1 toy	Y/N	Y/N	Y/N	Y/N	Y/N
1g	generalization	Y/N	Y/N	Y/N	Y/N	Y/N
2	uses at least 2 words for 1 toy	Y/N	Y/N	Y/N	Y/N	Y/N
2g	generalization	Y/N	Y/N	Y/N	Y/N	Y/N
3	uses at least 3 words for 1 toy	Y/N	Y/N	Y/N	Y/N	Y/N
3g	generalization	Y/N	Y/N	Y/N	Y/N	Y/N
4	uses at least 3 words for 2 different toys	Y/N	Y/N	Y/N	Y/N	Y/N
4g	generalization	Y/N	Y/N	Y/N	Y/N	Y/N
5	uses at least 5 words for 3 different toys	Y/N	Y/N	Y/N	Y/N	Y/N
5g	generalization	Y/N	Y/N	Y/N	Y/N	Y/N

Child Name: . . . .

Sings Songs

Teaching Procedure: Present the child with the direction: "LET'S SING _____ [NAME SONG]."

Materials: None.

	STEPS					
1	Itsy Bitsy Spider—hand movements only	Y/N	Y/N	Y/N	Y/N	Y/N
1a	Itsy Bitsy Spider—words if the child is verbal	Y/N	Y/N	Y/N	Y/N	Y/N
1g	generalization	Y/N	Y/N	Y/N	Y/N	Y/N
2	If You're Happy and You Know It—hand movements only	Y/N	Y/N	Y/N	Y/N	Y/N
2a	If You're Happy and You Know It—words if the child is verbal	Y/N	Y/N	Y/N	Y/N	Y/N
2g	generalization	Y/N	Y/N	Y/N	Y/N	Y/N
3	Head, Shoulder, Knees, and Toes—hand movements only	Y/N	Y/N	Y/N	Y/N	Y/N
3a	Head, Shoulder, Knees, and Toes—words if the child is verbal	Y/N	Y/N	Y/N	Y/N	Y/N
3g	generalization	Y/N	Y/N	Y/N	Y/N	Y/N

Child Name: . . . .

Games

Teaching Procedure: Present the child with the direction "LET'S PLAY ____ [NAME THE GAME]."

Materials: None.

Note: You need to teach both the words and actions with each step of duck duck goose. If the child is not verbal, then teach just the actions for both duck duck goose and ring around the rosy.

	STEPS					
1	duck duck goose	Y/N	Y/N	Y/N	Y/N	Y/N
1a	child sits while someone else gets picked as the goose	Y/N	Y/N	Y/N	Y/N	Y/N
1b	child is picked as the goose	Y/N	Y/N	Y/N	Y/N	Y/N
1c	child gets to be the one that walks around the circle and chooses the goose	Y/N	Y/N	Y/N	Y/N	Y/N
1g	generalization	Y/N	Y/N	Y/N	Y/N	Y/N
2	ring around the rosy	Y/N	Y/N	Y/N	Y/N	Y/N
2a	practice just the motions	Y/N	Y/N	Y/N	Y/N	Y/N
2b	learn the words	Y/N	Y/N	Y/N	Y/N	Y/N
2g	generalization	Y/N	Y/N	Y/N	Y/N	Y/N

Child Name: . . . .

Pretend Play

Teaching Procedure: Present the child with the direction "LET'S BE A ___ [NAME CHARACTER]."

Materials: Dress-up clothes of a policeman, fireman, princess, doctor, etc.

Note: Child will need to dress up like the character and act like them too.

	STEPS					
1	police man	Y/N	Y/N	Y/N	Y/N	Y/N
1g	generalization	Y/N	Y/N	Y/N	Y/N	Y/N
2	fireman	Y/N	Y/N	Y/N	Y/N	Y/N
2g	generalization	Y/N	Y/N	Y/N	Y/N	Y/N
3	doctor	Y/N	Y/N	Y/N	Y/N	Y/N
3g	generalization	Y/N	Y/N	Y/N	Y/N	Y/N
4	princess/action hero	Y/N	Y/N	Y/N	Y/N	Y/N
4g	generalization	Y/N	Y/N	Y/N	Y/N	Y/N

Self Help Programs

Child Name:. . . . .

Drinks from a Cup

Teaching Procedure: Present the child with the direction "DRINK/TAKE A SIP."

Materials: Cup with highly preferred liquid in it.

	STEPS					
1	will pick up the cup with 2 hands	Y/N	Y/N	Y/N	Y/N	Y/N
1g	generalization	Y/N	Y/N	Y/N	Y/N	Y/N
2	will put the cup to their mouth	Y/N	Y/N	Y/N	Y/N	Y/N
2g	generalization	Y/N	Y/N	Y/N	Y/N	Y/N
3	will take 1 sip out of the cup	Y/N	Y/N	Y/N	Y/N	Y/N
3g	generalization	Y/N	Y/N	Y/N	Y/N	Y/N
4	will put the cup back down	Y/N	Y/N	Y/N	Y/N	Y/N
4g	generalization	Y/N	Y/N	Y/N	Y/N	Y/N

Child Name: . . . .

Uses a Spoon

Teaching Procedure: Present the child with the direction "EAT."

Materials: Spoon, bowl, highly preferred edible that is easy to scoop up (yogurt, oatmeal).

	STEPS					
1	will pick up the spoon	Y/N	Y/N	Y/N	Y/N	Y/N
1g	generalization	Y/N	Y/N	Y/N	Y/N	Y/N
2	will take the spoon and scoop up the food	Y/N	Y/N	Y/N	Y/N	Y/N
2g	generalization	Y/N	Y/N	Y/N	Y/N	Y/N
3	will take the spoon and put it in their mouth	Y/N	Y/N	Y/N	Y/N	Y/N
3g	generalization	Y/N	Y/N	Y/N	Y/N	Y/N
4	will put the spoon down	Y/N	Y/N	Y/N	Y/N	Y/N
4g	generalization	Y/N	Y/N	Y/N	Y/N	Y/N

Child Name:. . . . .

Uses a Fork

Teaching Procedure: Present the child with the direction "EAT."

Materials: Fork, highly preferred edible that is easy to stab with a fork.

	STEPS					
1	will pick up the fork	Y/N	Y/N	Y/N	Y/N	Y/N
1g	generalization	Y/N	Y/N	Y/N	Y/N	Y/N
2	will take the fork and stab the edible	Y/N	Y/N	Y/N	Y/N	Y/N
2g	generalization	Y/N	Y/N	Y/N	Y/N	Y/N
3	will take the fork and put it in their mouth	Y/N	Y/N	Y/N	Y/N	Y/N
3g	generalization	Y/N	Y/N	Y/N	Y/N	Y/N
4	will put the fork down	Y/N	Y/N	Y/N	Y/N	Y/N
4g	generalization	Y/N	Y/N	Y/N	Y/N	Y/N

Child Name: . . . .

Getting Dressed: Shoes

Teaching Procedure: Present the child with the direction "PUT SHOES ON/TAKE SHOES OFF."
Materials: Shoes.
Note: Only work with Velcro shoes.

	STEPS					
1	can pull open the Velcro	Y/N	Y/N	Y/N	Y/N	Y/N
1g	generalization	Y/N	Y/N	Y/N	Y/N	Y/N
2	can take shoes off	Y/N	Y/N	Y/N	Y/N	Y/N
2g	generalization	Y/N	Y/N	Y/N	Y/N	Y/N
3	can put shoes on	Y/N	Y/N	Y/N	Y/N	Y/N
3g	generalization	Y/N	Y/N	Y/N	Y/N	Y/N
4	can close the Velcro	Y/N	Y/N	Y/N	Y/N	Y/N
4g	generalization	Y/N	Y/N	Y/N	Y/N	Y/N

Child Name: . . . .

Getting Dressed: Pants

Teaching Procedure: Present the child with the direction "PUT PANTS ON/TAKE PANTS OFF."

Materials: Pants.

Note: The child does not need to zipper or button the pants.

	STEPS					
1	can pull pants down	Y/N	Y/N	Y/N	Y/N	Y/N
1g	generalization	Y/N	Y/N	Y/N	Y/N	Y/N
2	can pull pants down and take both feet out	Y/N	Y/N	Y/N	Y/N	Y/N
2g	generalization	Y/N	Y/N	Y/N	Y/N	Y/N
3	can pull pants up	Y/N	Y/N	Y/N	Y/N	Y/N
3g	generalization	Y/N	Y/N	Y/N	Y/N	Y/N
4	can put both feet in the pants and pull them up	Y/N	Y/N	Y/N	Y/N	Y/N
4g	generalization	Y/N	Y/N	Y/N	Y/N	Y/N

Child Name: . . . .

Getting Dressed: Shirt

Teaching Procedure: Present the child with the direction: "PUT SHIRT ON/TAKE SHIRT OFF."
Materials: Shirt.

	STEPS					
1	can pull right arm out of sleeve	Y/N	Y/N	Y/N	Y/N	Y/N
1g	generalization	Y/N	Y/N	Y/N	Y/N	Y/N
2	can pull left arm out of sleeve	Y/N	Y/N	Y/N	Y/N	Y/N
2g	generalization	Y/N	Y/N	Y/N	Y/N	Y/N
3	can pull shirt over their head	Y/N	Y/N	Y/N	Y/N	Y/N
3g	generalization	Y/N	Y/N	Y/N	Y/N	Y/N
4	can pull shirt over their head (putting it back on)	Y/N	Y/N	Y/N	Y/N	Y/N
4g	generalization	Y/N	Y/N	Y/N	Y/N	Y/N
5	can put right arm in sleeve	Y/N	Y/N	Y/N	Y/N	Y/N
5g	generalization	Y/N	Y/N	Y/N	Y/N	Y/N
6	can put left arm in sleeve	Y/N	Y/N	Y/N	Y/N	Y/N
6g	generalization	Y/N	Y/N	Y/N	Y/N	Y/N

Child Name: ....

Wash Hands

Teaching Procedure: Present the child with the direction "WASH HANDS."

Materials: Sink, soap.

Note: This program should be taught using backwards chaining. This means that you will physically prompt the child through the entire sequence up until the last step. Once the last step is mastered, you will prompt the child through the sequence except the last 2 steps. This program is written so step 1 is the last step in the sequence.

	STEPS					
1	turn off water	Y/N	Y/N	Y/N	Y/N	Y/N
1g	generalization	Y/N	Y/N	Y/N	Y/N	Y/N
2	place both hands under the water until all soap is gone	Y/N	Y/N	Y/N	Y/N	Y/N
2g	generalization	Y/N	Y/N	Y/N	Y/N	Y/N
3	rub left palm to back of right hand	Y/N	Y/N	Y/N	Y/N	Y/N
3g	generalization	Y/N	Y/N	Y/N	Y/N	Y/N
4	rub right palm to back of left hand	Y/N	Y/N	Y/N	Y/N	Y/N
4g	generalization	Y/N	Y/N	Y/N	Y/N	Y/N
5	rub palms together	Y/N	Y/N	Y/N	Y/N	Y/N
5g	generalization	Y/N	Y/N	Y/N	Y/N	Y/N
6	get soap	Y/N	Y/N	Y/N	Y/N	Y/N
6g	generalization	Y/N	Y/N	Y/N	Y/N	Y/N
7	place hands under the water	Y/N	Y/N	Y/N	Y/N	Y/N
7g	generalization	Y/N	Y/N	Y/N	Y/N	Y/N
8	turn on cold water	Y/N	Y/N	Y/N	Y/N	Y/N
8g	generalization	Y/N	Y/N	Y/N	Y/N	Y/N

Child Name: . . . .

Dry Hands

Teaching Procedure: Present the child with the direction "DRY HANDS."

Materials: Towel.

Note: This program should be taught using backwards chaining. This means that you will physically prompt the child through the entire sequence up until the last step. Once the last step is mastered, you will prompt the child through the sequence except the last 2 steps. This program is written so step 1 is the last step in the sequence.

	STEPS					
1	throw out towel	Y/N	Y/N	Y/N	Y/N	Y/N
1g	generalization	Y/N	Y/N	Y/N	Y/N	Y/N
2	dry the back of the right hand	Y/N	Y/N	Y/N	Y/N	Y/N
2g	generalization	Y/N	Y/N	Y/N	Y/N	Y/N
3	dry the back of the left hand	Y/N	Y/N	Y/N	Y/N	Y/N
3g	generalization	Y/N	Y/N	Y/N	Y/N	Y/N
4	dry the palms of both hands	Y/N	Y/N	Y/N	Y/N	Y/N
4g	generalization	Y/N	Y/N	Y/N	Y/N	Y/N
5	get paper towel	Y/N	Y/N	Y/N	Y/N	Y/N
5g	generalization	Y/N	Y/N	Y/N	Y/N	Y/N

Sort/Match Programs

Child Name: . . . .

Match Identical Picture to Picture

Teaching Procedure: Present the child with the direction "MATCH" and follow the steps below.

Materials: Any common picture to picture can be used. Some suggestions are: car, animal, plate, utensils, clothing, brush, cup, book.

Note: Example of step 2 (match 2 different pictures to pictures in a field of 2). Lay down a picture of a cow and a car. Present the child with 2 pictures (1 of a cow and 1 of a car). Tell the child to match.

	STEPS					
1	will match a picture to picture in a field of 1	Y/N	Y/N	Y/N	Y/N	Y/N
1g	generalization—1 picture to picture in a field of 1 with 3 different people in 3 different settings	Y/N	Y/N	Y/N	Y/N	Y/N
2	will match 2 different pictures to pictures in a field of 2	Y/N	Y/N	Y/N	Y/N	Y/N
2g	generalization—up to 2 different pictures to pictures in a field of 2 with 3 different people in 3 different settings	Y/N	Y/N	Y/N	Y/N	Y/N
3	will match 3 different pictures to pictures in a field of 3	Y/N	Y/N	Y/N	Y/N	Y/N
3g	generalization—up to 3 different pictures to pictures in a field of 3 or more with 3 different people in 3 different settings	Y/N	Y/N	Y/N	Y/N	Y/N
4	will match up to 4 different pictures to pictures in a field of 3 or more	Y/N	Y/N	Y/N	Y/N	Y/N
4g	generalization—up to 4 different pictures to pictures in a field of 3 or more with 3 different people in 3 different settings	Y/N	Y/N	Y/N	Y/N	Y/N
5	will match up to 5 different pictures to pictures in a field of 3 or more	Y/N	Y/N	Y/N	Y/N	Y/N

5g	generalization—up to 5 different pictures to pictures in a field of 3 or more with 3 different people in 3 different settings	Y/N	Y/N	Y/N	Y/N	Y/N
6	will match up to 6 different pictures to pictures in a field of 3 or more	Y/N	Y/N	Y/N	Y/N	Y/N
6g	generalization—up to 6 different pictures to pictures in a field of 3 or more with 3 different people in 3 different settings	Y/N	Y/N	Y/N	Y/N	Y/N
7	will match up to 7 different pictures to pictures in a field of 3 or more	Y/N	Y/N	Y/N	Y/N	Y/N
7g	generalization—up to 7 different pictures to pictures in a field of 3 or more with 3 different people in 3 different settings	Y/N	Y/N	Y/N	Y/N	Y/N
8	will match up to 8 different pictures to pictures in a field of 3 or more	Y/N	Y/N	Y/N	Y/N	Y/N
8g	generalization—up to 8 different pictures to pictures in a field of 3 or more with 3 different people in 3 different settings	Y/N	Y/N	Y/N	Y/N	Y/N
9	will match up to 9 different pictures to pictures in a field of 3 or more	Y/N	Y/N	Y/N	Y/N	Y/N
9g	generalization—up to 9 different pictures to pictures in a field of 3 or more with 3 different people in 3 different settings	Y/N	Y/N	Y/N	Y/N	Y/N
10	will match up to 10 different pictures to pictures in a field of 3 or more	Y/N	Y/N	Y/N	Y/N	Y/N
10g	generalization—up to 10 different pictures to pictures in a field of 3 or more with 3 different people in 3 different settings	Y/N	Y/N	Y/N	Y/N	Y/N

Child Name: . . . .

Match Identical Object to Object

Teaching Procedure: Present the child with the direction "MATCH" and follow the steps below.

Materials: Any common object to object can be used. Some suggestions are: car, animal, plate, utensils, clothing, brush, cup, book.

Note: Example of step 2 (match 2 different objects to objects in a field of 2). Lay down an object of a cow and a car. Present the child with 2 objects (1 a cow and 1 a car). Tell the child to match.

	STEPS					
1	will match an object to object in a field of 1	Y/N	Y/N	Y/N	Y/N	Y/N
1g	generalization—1 object to object in a field of 1 with 3 different people in 3 different settings	Y/N	Y/N	Y/N	Y/N	Y/N
2	will match 2 different objects to objects in a field of 2	Y/N	Y/N	Y/N	Y/N	Y/N
2g	generalization—up to 2 different objects to objects in a field of 2 with 3 different people in 3 different settings	Y/N	Y/N	Y/N	Y/N	Y/N
3	will match 3 different objects to objects in a field of 3	Y/N	Y/N	Y/N	Y/N	Y/N
3g	generalization—up to 3 different objects to objects in a field of 3 or more with 3 different people in 3 different settings	Y/N	Y/N	Y/N	Y/N	Y/N
4	will match up to 4 different objects to objects in a field of 3 or more	Y/N	Y/N	Y/N	Y/N	Y/N
4g	generalization—up to 4 different objects to objects in a field of 3 or more with 3 different people in 3 different settings	Y/N	Y/N	Y/N	Y/N	Y/N
5	will match up to 5 different objects to objects in a field of 3 or more	Y/N	Y/N	Y/N	Y/N	Y/N

5g	generalization—up to 5 different objects to objects in a field of 3 or more with 3 different people in 3 different settings	Y/N	Y/N	Y/N	Y/N	Y/N
6	will match up to 6 different objects to objects in a field of 3 or more	Y/N	Y/N	Y/N	Y/N	Y/N
6g	generalization—up to 6 different objects to objects in a field of 3 or more with 3 different people in 3 different settings	Y/N	Y/N	Y/N	Y/N	Y/N
7	will match up to 7 different objects to objects in a field of 3 or more	Y/N	Y/N	Y/N	Y/N	Y/N
7g	generalization—up to 7 different objects to objects in a field of 3 or more with 3 different people in 3 different settings	Y/N	Y/N	Y/N	Y/N	Y/N
8	will match up to 8 different objects to objects in a field of 3 or more	Y/N	Y/N	Y/N	Y/N	Y/N
8g	generalization—up to 8 different objects to objects in a field of 3 or more with 3 different people in 3 different settings	Y/N	Y/N	Y/N	Y/N	Y/N
9	will match up to 9 different objects to objects in a field of 3 or more	Y/N	Y/N	Y/N	Y/N	Y/N
9g	generalization—up to 9 different objects to objects in a field of 3 or more with 3 different people in 3 different settings	Y/N	Y/N	Y/N	Y/N	Y/N
10	will match up to 10 different objects to objects in a field of 3 or more	Y/N	Y/N	Y/N	Y/N	Y/N
10g	generalization—up to 10 different objects to objects in a field of 3 or more with 3 different people in 3 different settings	Y/N	Y/N	Y/N	Y/N	Y/N

Child Name: . . . .

Match Object to Picture

Teaching Procedure: Present the child with the direction "MATCH" and follow the steps below.

Materials: You will need common objects that correspond to the same pictures. Some examples are: car, animal, furniture, ball, crayon, utensil, clothing.

Note: Example of step 2 (match 2 different objects to pictures in a field of 2). Lay down a picture of a cow and a car. Present the child with 2 objects (1 a cow and 1 a car). Tell the child to match.

	STEPS					
1	will match an object to a picture in a field of 1	Y/N	Y/N	Y/N	Y/N	Y/N
1g	generalization—1 object to a picture in a field of 1 with 3 different people in 3 different settings	Y/N	Y/N	Y/N	Y/N	Y/N
2	will match 2 different objects to pictures in a field of 2	Y/N	Y/N	Y/N	Y/N	Y/N
2g	generalization—up to 2 different objects to pictures in a field of 2 with 3 different people in 3 different settings	Y/N	Y/N	Y/N	Y/N	Y/N
3	will match 3 different objects to pictures in a field of 3	Y/N	Y/N	Y/N	Y/N	Y/N
3g	generalization—up to 3 different objects to pictures in a field of 3 or more with 3 different people in 3 different settings	Y/N	Y/N	Y/N	Y/N	Y/N
4	will match up to 4 different objects to pictures in a field of 3 or more	Y/N	Y/N	Y/N	Y/N	Y/N
4g	generalization—up to 4 different objects to pictures in a field of 3 or more with 3 different people in 3 different settings	Y/N	Y/N	Y/N	Y/N	Y/N
5	will match up to 5 different objects to pictures in a field of 3 or more	Y/N	Y/N	Y/N	Y/N	Y/N

5g	generalization—up to 5 different objects to pictures in a field of 3 or more with 3 different people in 3 different settings	Y/N	Y/N	Y/N	Y/N	Y/N
6	will match up to 6 different objects to pictures in a field of 3 or more	Y/N	Y/N	Y/N	Y/N	Y/N
6g	generalization—up to 6 different objects in a field of 3 or more with 3 different people in 3 different settings	Y/N	Y/N	Y/N	Y/N	Y/N
7	will match up to 7 different objects to pictures in a field of 3 or more	Y/N	Y/N	Y/N	Y/N	Y/N
7g	generalization—up to 7 different objects to pictures in a field of 3 or more with 3 different people in 3 different settings	Y/N	Y/N	Y/N	Y/N	Y/N
8	will match up to 8 different objects to pictures in a field of 3 or more	Y/N	Y/N	Y/N	Y/N	Y/N
8g	generalization—up to 8 different objects in a field of 3 or more with 3 different people in 3 different settings	Y/N	Y/N	Y/N	Y/N	Y/N
9	will match up to 9 different objects to pictures in a field of 3 or more	Y/N	Y/N	Y/N	Y/N	Y/N
9g	generalization—up to 9 different objects in a field of 3 or more with 3 different people in 3 different settings	Y/N	Y/N	Y/N	Y/N	Y/N
10	will match up to 10 different objects to pictures in a field of 3 or more	Y/N	Y/N	Y/N	Y/N	Y/N
10g	generalization—up to 10 different objects to pictures in a field of 3 or more with 3 different people in 3 different settings	Y/N	Y/N	Y/N	Y/N	Y/N

Child Name: . . . .

Sort Identical Items

Teaching Procedure: For steps 1–5: lay down 3 non-identical items but all from the same category (e.g. colors); give the child the matching items and ask them to sort. For example, lay down purple, red, and blue on the table. Give the child 2 purples, 2 reds, and 2 blues (at least 2) and ask them to sort. For step 6: lay down on table at least 3 different categories (clothing, utensil, shape) and give the child at least 2 items from each category and ask them to sort. For example, on the table is a shoe, fork, and square. Give the child 2 shoes, 2 forks, and 2 squares and tell them to sort.

Materials: Same exact animals, utensils, colors, shapes, clothes.

	STEPS					
1	in a field of 3 can sort identical colors (e.g. red to red, blue to blue, purple to purple)	Y/N	Y/N	Y/N	Y/N	Y/N
1g	generalization	Y/N	Y/N	Y/N	Y/N	Y/N
2	in a field of 3 can sort identical animals (e.g. tiger to tiger, lion to lion, dog to dog)	Y/N	Y/N	Y/N	Y/N	Y/N
2g	generalization	Y/N	Y/N	Y/N	Y/N	Y/N
3	in a field of 3 can sort identical shapes	Y/N	Y/N	Y/N	Y/N	Y/N
3g	generalization	Y/N	Y/N	Y/N	Y/N	Y/N
4	in a field of 3 can sort identical utensils	Y/N	Y/N	Y/N	Y/N	Y/N
4g	generalization	Y/N	Y/N	Y/N	Y/N	Y/N
5	in a field of 3 can sort identical articles of clothing	Y/N	Y/N	Y/N	Y/N	Y/N
5g	generalization	Y/N	Y/N	Y/N	Y/N	Y/N
6	in a field of 3 or more, sort identical items from different categories	Y/N	Y/N	Y/N	Y/N	Y/N
6g	generalization	Y/N	Y/N	Y/N	Y/N	Y/N

Child Name:. . . . .

Sort Non-Identical Items

Teaching Procedure: Lay down 3 (or more, depending on the step) non-identical items: car, color, article of clothing. Present the child with 2 or more items from each category and ask them to sort. The items should be from the same category but not identical items. For example, car, blue, and shirt are on the table. Give the child 2 (or more) non-identical vehicles, 2 (or more) colors, and 2 (or more) articles of clothing and tell the child to sort.

Materials: Animals, utensils, colors, shapes, clothes, books, dolls, cars.

	STEPS					
1	in a field of 3 can sort non-identical items	Y/N	Y/N	Y/N	Y/N	Y/N
1g	generalization	Y/N	Y/N	Y/N	Y/N	Y/N
2	in a field of 5 can sort non-identical items	Y/N	Y/N	Y/N	Y/N	Y/N
2g	generalization	Y/N	Y/N	Y/N	Y/N	Y/N
3	in a field of 8 can sort non-identical items	Y/N	Y/N	Y/N	Y/N	Y/N
3g	generalization	Y/N	Y/N	Y/N	Y/N	Y/N

Academic Programs

Child Name: . . . .

Receptive Identification of Colors

Teaching Procedure: In a field of 3 or more ask the child to "POINT/TOUCH/SHOW ME ___ [NAME THE COLOR]."

Materials: Various colors on different backgrounds.

	STEPS					
1	blue	Y/N	Y/N	Y/N	Y/N	Y/N
1g	generalization	Y/N	Y/N	Y/N	Y/N	Y/N
2	green	Y/N	Y/N	Y/N	Y/N	Y/N
2g	generalization	Y/N	Y/N	Y/N	Y/N	Y/N
3	red	Y/N	Y/N	Y/N	Y/N	Y/N
3g	generalization	Y/N	Y/N	Y/N	Y/N	Y/N
4	purple	Y/N	Y/N	Y/N	Y/N	Y/N
4g	generalization	Y/N	Y/N	Y/N	Y/N	Y/N
5	orange	Y/N	Y/N	Y/N	Y/N	Y/N
5g	generalization	Y/N	Y/N	Y/N	Y/N	Y/N
6	yellow	Y/N	Y/N	Y/N	Y/N	Y/N
6g	generalization	Y/N	Y/N	Y/N	Y/N	Y/N
7	brown	Y/N	Y/N	Y/N	Y/N	Y/N
7g	generalization	Y/N	Y/N	Y/N	Y/N	Y/N
8	black	Y/N	Y/N	Y/N	Y/N	Y/N
8g	generalization	Y/N	Y/N	Y/N	Y/N	Y/N
9	white	Y/N	Y/N	Y/N	Y/N	Y/N
9g	generalization	Y/N	Y/N	Y/N	Y/N	Y/N
10	pink	Y/N	Y/N	Y/N	Y/N	Y/N
10g	generalization	Y/N	Y/N	Y/N	Y/N	Y/N

Child Name: . . . .

Expressive Identification of Colors

Teaching Procedure: Hold up the color and ask the child "WHAT IS IT?"
Materials: Various colors.

	STEPS					
1	blue	Y/N	Y/N	Y/N	Y/N	Y/N
1g	generalization	Y/N	Y/N	Y/N	Y/N	Y/N
2	green	Y/N	Y/N	Y/N	Y/N	Y/N
2g	generalization	Y/N	Y/N	Y/N	Y/N	Y/N
3	red	Y/N	Y/N	Y/N	Y/N	Y/N
3g	generalization	Y/N	Y/N	Y/N	Y/N	Y/N
4	purple	Y/N	Y/N	Y/N	Y/N	Y/N
4g	generalization	Y/N	Y/N	Y/N	Y/N	Y/N
5	orange	Y/N	Y/N	Y/N	Y/N	Y/N
5g	generalization	Y/N	Y/N	Y/N	Y/N	Y/N
6	yellow	Y/N	Y/N	Y/N	Y/N	Y/N
6g	generalization	Y/N	Y/N	Y/N	Y/N	Y/N
7	brown	Y/N	Y/N	Y/N	Y/N	Y/N
7g	generalization	Y/N	Y/N	Y/N	Y/N	Y/N
8	black	Y/N	Y/N	Y/N	Y/N	Y/N
8g	generalization	Y/N	Y/N	Y/N	Y/N	Y/N
9	white	Y/N	Y/N	Y/N	Y/N	Y/N
9g	generalization	Y/N	Y/N	Y/N	Y/N	Y/N
10	pink	Y/N	Y/N	Y/N	Y/N	Y/N
10g	generalization	Y/N	Y/N	Y/N	Y/N	Y/N

Child Name: . . . .

Receptive Identification of Shapes

Teaching Procedure: In a field of 3 or more ask the child to "POINT/TOUCH/SHOW ME ___ [NAME THE SHAPE]."

Materials: Various shapes on different backgrounds.

	STEPS					
1	circle	Y/N	Y/N	Y/N	Y/N	Y/N
1g	generalization	Y/N	Y/N	Y/N	Y/N	Y/N
2	square	Y/N	Y/N	Y/N	Y/N	Y/N
2g	generalization	Y/N	Y/N	Y/N	Y/N	Y/N
3	triangle	Y/N	Y/N	Y/N	Y/N	Y/N
3g	generalization	Y/N	Y/N	Y/N	Y/N	Y/N
4	rectangle	Y/N	Y/N	Y/N	Y/N	Y/N
4g	generalization	Y/N	Y/N	Y/N	Y/N	Y/N
5	oval	Y/N	Y/N	Y/N	Y/N	Y/N
5g	generalization	Y/N	Y/N	Y/N	Y/N	Y/N
6	star	Y/N	Y/N	Y/N	Y/N	Y/N
6g	generalization	Y/N	Y/N	Y/N	Y/N	Y/N

Child Name: . . . .

Expressive Identification of Shapes

Teaching Procedure: Hold up the shape and ask the child "WHAT SHAPE IS IT?"
Materials: Various shapes.

	STEPS					
1	circle	Y/N	Y/N	Y/N	Y/N	Y/N
1g	generalization	Y/N	Y/N	Y/N	Y/N	Y/N
2	square	Y/N	Y/N	Y/N	Y/N	Y/N
2g	generalization	Y/N	Y/N	Y/N	Y/N	Y/N
3	triangle	Y/N	Y/N	Y/N	Y/N	Y/N
3g	generalization	Y/N	Y/N	Y/N	Y/N	Y/N
4	rectangle	Y/N	Y/N	Y/N	Y/N	Y/N
4g	generalization	Y/N	Y/N	Y/N	Y/N	Y/N
5	oval	Y/N	Y/N	Y/N	Y/N	Y/N
5g	generalization	Y/N	Y/N	Y/N	Y/N	Y/N
6	star	Y/N	Y/N	Y/N	Y/N	Y/N
6g	generalization	Y/N	Y/N	Y/N	Y/N	Y/N

Child Name: . . . .

Receptive Identification of Upper Case Letters

Teaching Procedure: In a field of 3 or more lay out cards/pictures of individual letters, present the child with the direction "TOUCH/POINT TO/FIND ___ [LETTER]."

Materials: Various letters in different fonts and colors, and on different types of card.

	STEPS					
1	A	Y/N	Y/N	Y/N	Y/N	Y/N
1g	generalization	Y/N	Y/N	Y/N	Y/N	Y/N
2	B	Y/N	Y/N	Y/N	Y/N	Y/N
2g	generalization	Y/N	Y/N	Y/N	Y/N	Y/N
3	C	Y/N	Y/N	Y/N	Y/N	Y/N
3g	generalization	Y/N	Y/N	Y/N	Y/N	Y/N
4	D	Y/N	Y/N	Y/N	Y/N	Y/N
4g	generalization	Y/N	Y/N	Y/N	Y/N	Y/N
5	E	Y/N	Y/N	Y/N	Y/N	Y/N
5g	generalization	Y/N	Y/N	Y/N	Y/N	Y/N
6	F	Y/N	Y/N	Y/N	Y/N	Y/N
6g	generalization	Y/N	Y/N	Y/N	Y/N	Y/N
7	G	Y/N	Y/N	Y/N	Y/N	Y/N
7g	generalization	Y/N	Y/N	Y/N	Y/N	Y/N
8	H	Y/N	Y/N	Y/N	Y/N	Y/N
8g	generalization	Y/N	Y/N	Y/N	Y/N	Y/N
9	I	Y/N	Y/N	Y/N	Y/N	Y/N
9g	generalization	Y/N	Y/N	Y/N	Y/N	Y/N
10	J	Y/N	Y/N	Y/N	Y/N	Y/N
10g	generalization	Y/N	Y/N	Y/N	Y/N	Y/N
11	K	Y/N	Y/N	Y/N	Y/N	Y/N
11g	generalization	Y/N	Y/N	Y/N	Y/N	Y/N
12	L	Y/N	Y/N	Y/N	Y/N	Y/N

12g	generalization	Y/N	Y/N	Y/N	Y/N	Y/N
13	M	Y/N	Y/N	Y/N	Y/N	Y/N
13g	generalization	Y/N	Y/N	Y/N	Y/N	Y/N
14	N	Y/N	Y/N	Y/N	Y/N	Y/N
14g	generalization	Y/N	Y/N	Y/N	Y/N	Y/N
15	O	Y/N	Y/N	Y/N	Y/N	Y/N
15g	generalization	Y/N	Y/N	Y/N	Y/N	Y/N
16	P	Y/N	Y/N	Y/N	Y/N	Y/N
16g	generalization	Y/N	Y/N	Y/N	Y/N	Y/N
17	Q	Y/N	Y/N	Y/N	Y/N	Y/N
17g	generalization	Y/N	Y/N	Y/N	Y/N	Y/N
18	R	Y/N	Y/N	Y/N	Y/N	Y/N
18g	generalization	Y/N	Y/N	Y/N	Y/N	Y/N
19	S	Y/N	Y/N	Y/N	Y/N	Y/N
19g	generalization	Y/N	Y/N	Y/N	Y/N	Y/N
20	T	Y/N	Y/N	Y/N	Y/N	Y/N
20g	generalization	Y/N	Y/N	Y/N	Y/N	Y/N
21	U	Y/N	Y/N	Y/N	Y/N	Y/N
21g	generalization	Y/N	Y/N	Y/N	Y/N	Y/N
22	V	Y/N	Y/N	Y/N	Y/N	Y/N
22g	generalization	Y/N	Y/N	Y/N	Y/N	Y/N
23	W	Y/N	Y/N	Y/N	Y/N	Y/N
23g	generalization	Y/N	Y/N	Y/N	Y/N	Y/N
24	X	Y/N	Y/N	Y/N	Y/N	Y/N
24g	generalization	Y/N	Y/N	Y/N	Y/N	Y/N
25	Y	Y/N	Y/N	Y/N	Y/N	Y/N
25g	generalization	Y/N	Y/N	Y/N	Y/N	Y/N
26	Z	Y/N	Y/N	Y/N	Y/N	Y/N
26g	generalization	Y/N	Y/N	Y/N	Y/N	Y/N

Child Name:. . . . .

Receptive Identification of Lower Case Letters

Teaching Procedure: In a field of 3 or more lay out cards/pictures of individual letters; present the child with the direction "TOUCH/FIND/POINT TO ___ [LETTER]."

Materials: Various letters in different fonts and colors, and on different types of card.

	STEPS					
1	a	Y/N	Y/N	Y/N	Y/N	Y/N
1g	generalization	Y/N	Y/N	Y/N	Y/N	Y/N
2	b	Y/N	Y/N	Y/N	Y/N	Y/N
2g	generalization	Y/N	Y/N	Y/N	Y/N	Y/N
3	c	Y/N	Y/N	Y/N	Y/N	Y/N
3g	generalization	Y/N	Y/N	Y/N	Y/N	Y/N
4	d	Y/N	Y/N	Y/N	Y/N	Y/N
4g	generalization	Y/N	Y/N	Y/N	Y/N	Y/N
5	e	Y/N	Y/N	Y/N	Y/N	Y/N
5g	generalization	Y/N	Y/N	Y/N	Y/N	Y/N
6	f	Y/N	Y/N	Y/N	Y/N	Y/N
6g	generalization	Y/N	Y/N	Y/N	Y/N	Y/N
7	g	Y/N	Y/N	Y/N	Y/N	Y/N
7g	generalization	Y/N	Y/N	Y/N	Y/N	Y/N
8	h	Y/N	Y/N	Y/N	Y/N	Y/N
8g	generalization	Y/N	Y/N	Y/N	Y/N	Y/N
9	i	Y/N	Y/N	Y/N	Y/N	Y/N
9g	generalization	Y/N	Y/N	Y/N	Y/N	Y/N
10	j	Y/N	Y/N	Y/N	Y/N	Y/N
10g	generalization	Y/N	Y/N	Y/N	Y/N	Y/N
11	k	Y/N	Y/N	Y/N	Y/N	Y/N
11g	generalization	Y/N	Y/N	Y/N	Y/N	Y/N
12	l	Y/N	Y/N	Y/N	Y/N	Y/N

12g	generalization	Y/N	Y/N	Y/N	Y/N	Y/N
13	m	Y/N	Y/N	Y/N	Y/N	Y/N
13g	generalization	Y/N	Y/N	Y/N	Y/N	Y/N
14	n	Y/N	Y/N	Y/N	Y/N	Y/N
14g	generalization	Y/N	Y/N	Y/N	Y/N	Y/N
15	o	Y/N	Y/N	Y/N	Y/N	Y/N
15g	generalization	Y/N	Y/N	Y/N	Y/N	Y/N
16	p	Y/N	Y/N	Y/N	Y/N	Y/N
16g	generalization	Y/N	Y/N	Y/N	Y/N	Y/N
17	q	Y/N	Y/N	Y/N	Y/N	Y/N
17g	generalization	Y/N	Y/N	Y/N	Y/N	Y/N
18	r	Y/N	Y/N	Y/N	Y/N	Y/N
18g	generalization	Y/N	Y/N	Y/N	Y/N	Y/N
19	s	Y/N	Y/N	Y/N	Y/N	Y/N
19g	generalization	Y/N	Y/N	Y/N	Y/N	Y/N
20	t	Y/N	Y/N	Y/N	Y/N	Y/N
20g	generalization	Y/N	Y/N	Y/N	Y/N	Y/N
21	u	Y/N	Y/N	Y/N	Y/N	Y/N
21g	generalization	Y/N	Y/N	Y/N	Y/N	Y/N
22	v	Y/N	Y/N	Y/N	Y/N	Y/N
22g	generalization	Y/N	Y/N	Y/N	Y/N	Y/N
23	w	Y/N	Y/N	Y/N	Y/N	Y/N
23g	generalization	Y/N	Y/N	Y/N	Y/N	Y/N
24	x	Y/N	Y/N	Y/N	Y/N	Y/N
24g	generalization	Y/N	Y/N	Y/N	Y/N	Y/N
25	y	Y/N	Y/N	Y/N	Y/N	Y/N
25g	generalization	Y/N	Y/N	Y/N	Y/N	Y/N
26	z	Y/N	Y/N	Y/N	Y/N	Y/N
26g	generalization	Y/N	Y/N	Y/N	Y/N	Y/N

Child Name:. . . . .

Expressive Identification of Upper Case Letters

Teaching Procedure: Hold up the letter and ask the child "WHAT LETTER IS IT?"

Materials: Various letters in different fonts and colors, and on different types of card.

	STEPS					
1	A	Y/N	Y/N	Y/N	Y/N	Y/N
1g	generalization	Y/N	Y/N	Y/N	Y/N	Y/N
2	B	Y/N	Y/N	Y/N	Y/N	Y/N
2g	generalization	Y/N	Y/N	Y/N	Y/N	Y/N
3	C	Y/N	Y/N	Y/N	Y/N	Y/N
3g	generalization	Y/N	Y/N	Y/N	Y/N	Y/N
4	D	Y/N	Y/N	Y/N	Y/N	Y/N
4g	generalization	Y/N	Y/N	Y/N	Y/N	Y/N
5	E	Y/N	Y/N	Y/N	Y/N	Y/N
5g	generalization	Y/N	Y/N	Y/N	Y/N	Y/N
6	F	Y/N	Y/N	Y/N	Y/N	Y/N
6g	generalization	Y/N	Y/N	Y/N	Y/N	Y/N
7	G	Y/N	Y/N	Y/N	Y/N	Y/N
7g	generalization	Y/N	Y/N	Y/N	Y/N	Y/N
8	H	Y/N	Y/N	Y/N	Y/N	Y/N
8g	generalization	Y/N	Y/N	Y/N	Y/N	Y/N
9	I	Y/N	Y/N	Y/N	Y/N	Y/N
9g	generalization	Y/N	Y/N	Y/N	Y/N	Y/N
10	J	Y/N	Y/N	Y/N	Y/N	Y/N
10g	generalization	Y/N	Y/N	Y/N	Y/N	Y/N
11	K	Y/N	Y/N	Y/N	Y/N	Y/N
11g	generalization	Y/N	Y/N	Y/N	Y/N	Y/N
12	L	Y/N	Y/N	Y/N	Y/N	Y/N

12g	generalization	Y/N	Y/N	Y/N	Y/N	Y/N
13	M	Y/N	Y/N	Y/N	Y/N	Y/N
13g	generalization	Y/N	Y/N	Y/N	Y/N	Y/N
14	N	Y/N	Y/N	Y/N	Y/N	Y/N
14g	generalization	Y/N	Y/N	Y/N	Y/N	Y/N
15	O	Y/N	Y/N	Y/N	Y/N	Y/N
15g	generalization	Y/N	Y/N	Y/N	Y/N	Y/N
16	P	Y/N	Y/N	Y/N	Y/N	Y/N
16g	generalization	Y/N	Y/N	Y/N	Y/N	Y/N
17	Q	Y/N	Y/N	Y/N	Y/N	Y/N
17g	generalization	Y/N	Y/N	Y/N	Y/N	Y/N
18	R	Y/N	Y/N	Y/N	Y/N	Y/N
18g	generalization	Y/N	Y/N	Y/N	Y/N	Y/N
19	S	Y/N	Y/N	Y/N	Y/N	Y/N
19g	generalization	Y/N	Y/N	Y/N	Y/N	Y/N
20	T	Y/N	Y/N	Y/N	Y/N	Y/N
20g	generalization	Y/N	Y/N	Y/N	Y/N	Y/N
21	U	Y/N	Y/N	Y/N	Y/N	Y/N
21g	generalization	Y/N	Y/N	Y/N	Y/N	Y/N
22	V	Y/N	Y/N	Y/N	Y/N	Y/N
22g	generalization	Y/N	Y/N	Y/N	Y/N	Y/N
23	W	Y/N	Y/N	Y/N	Y/N	Y/N
23g	generalization	Y/N	Y/N	Y/N	Y/N	Y/N
24	X	Y/N	Y/N	Y/N	Y/N	Y/N
24g	generalization	Y/N	Y/N	Y/N	Y/N	Y/N
25	Y	Y/N	Y/N	Y/N	Y/N	Y/N
25g	generalization	Y/N	Y/N	Y/N	Y/N	Y/N
26	Z	Y/N	Y/N	Y/N	Y/N	Y/N
26g	generalization	Y/N	Y/N	Y/N	Y/N	Y/N

Child Name:. . . . .

Expressive Identification of Lower Case Letters

Teaching Procedure: Hold up the letter and ask the child "WHAT LETTER IS IT?"

Materials: Various letters in different fonts and colors, and on different types of card.

	STEPS					
1	a	Y/N	Y/N	Y/N	Y/N	Y/N
1g	generalization	Y/N	Y/N	Y/N	Y/N	Y/N
2	b	Y/N	Y/N	Y/N	Y/N	Y/N
2g	generalization	Y/N	Y/N	Y/N	Y/N	Y/N
3	c	Y/N	Y/N	Y/N	Y/N	Y/N
3g	generalization	Y/N	Y/N	Y/N	Y/N	Y/N
4	d	Y/N	Y/N	Y/N	Y/N	Y/N
4g	generalization	Y/N	Y/N	Y/N	Y/N	Y/N
5	e	Y/N	Y/N	Y/N	Y/N	Y/N
5g	generalization	Y/N	Y/N	Y/N	Y/N	Y/N
6	f	Y/N	Y/N	Y/N	Y/N	Y/N
6g	generalization	Y/N	Y/N	Y/N	Y/N	Y/N
7	g	Y/N	Y/N	Y/N	Y/N	Y/N
7g	generalization	Y/N	Y/N	Y/N	Y/N	Y/N
8	h	Y/N	Y/N	Y/N	Y/N	Y/N
8g	generalization	Y/N	Y/N	Y/N	Y/N	Y/N
9	i	Y/N	Y/N	Y/N	Y/N	Y/N
9g	generalization	Y/N	Y/N	Y/N	Y/N	Y/N
10	j	Y/N	Y/N	Y/N	Y/N	Y/N
10g	generalization	Y/N	Y/N	Y/N	Y/N	Y/N
11	k	Y/N	Y/N	Y/N	Y/N	Y/N
11g	generalization	Y/N	Y/N	Y/N	Y/N	Y/N
12	l	Y/N	Y/N	Y/N	Y/N	Y/N

12g	generalization	Y/N	Y/N	Y/N	Y/N	Y/N
13	m	Y/N	Y/N	Y/N	Y/N	Y/N
13g	generalization	Y/N	Y/N	Y/N	Y/N	Y/N
14	n	Y/N	Y/N	Y/N	Y/N	Y/N
14g	generalization	Y/N	Y/N	Y/N	Y/N	Y/N
15	o	Y/N	Y/N	Y/N	Y/N	Y/N
15g	generalization	Y/N	Y/N	Y/N	Y/N	Y/N
16	p	Y/N	Y/N	Y/N	Y/N	Y/N
16g	generalization	Y/N	Y/N	Y/N	Y/N	Y/N
17	q	Y/N	Y/N	Y/N	Y/N	Y/N
17g	generalization	Y/N	Y/N	Y/N	Y/N	Y/N
18	r	Y/N	Y/N	Y/N	Y/N	Y/N
18g	generalization	Y/N	Y/N	Y/N	Y/N	Y/N
19	s	Y/N	Y/N	Y/N	Y/N	Y/N
19g	generalization	Y/N	Y/N	Y/N	Y/N	Y/N
20	t	Y/N	Y/N	Y/N	Y/N	Y/N
20g	generalization	Y/N	Y/N	Y/N	Y/N	Y/N
21	u	Y/N	Y/N	Y/N	Y/N	Y/N
21g	generalization	Y/N	Y/N	Y/N	Y/N	Y/N
22	v	Y/N	Y/N	Y/N	Y/N	Y/N
22g	generalization	Y/N	Y/N	Y/N	Y/N	Y/N
23	w	Y/N	Y/N	Y/N	Y/N	Y/N
23g	generalization	Y/N	Y/N	Y/N	Y/N	Y/N
24	x	Y/N	Y/N	Y/N	Y/N	Y/N
24g	generalization	Y/N	Y/N	Y/N	Y/N	Y/N
25	y	Y/N	Y/N	Y/N	Y/N	Y/N
25g	generalization	Y/N	Y/N	Y/N	Y/N	Y/N
26	z	Y/N	Y/N	Y/N	Y/N	Y/N
26g	generalization	Y/N	Y/N	Y/N	Y/N	Y/N

Child Name:. . . . .

Rote Counting

Teaching Procedure: Present the child with the direction "COUNT TO ___ [NAME THE NUMBER]."

Materials: None.

	STEPS					
1	can count to 5	Y/N	Y/N	Y/N	Y/N	Y/N
1g	generalization	Y/N	Y/N	Y/N	Y/N	Y/N
2	can count to 10	Y/N	Y/N	Y/N	Y/N	Y/N
2g	generalization	Y/N	Y/N	Y/N	Y/N	Y/N
3	can count to 15	Y/N	Y/N	Y/N	Y/N	Y/N
3g	generalization	Y/N	Y/N	Y/N	Y/N	Y/N
4	can count to 20	Y/N	Y/N	Y/N	Y/N	Y/N
4g	generalization	Y/N	Y/N	Y/N	Y/N	Y/N
5	can count to 25	Y/N	Y/N	Y/N	Y/N	Y/N
5g	generalization	Y/N	Y/N	Y/N	Y/N	Y/N
6	can count to 30	Y/N	Y/N	Y/N	Y/N	Y/N
6g	generalization	Y/N	Y/N	Y/N	Y/N	Y/N

Child Name: . . . .

Counting Objects

Teaching Procedure: Present the child with the direction "COUNT."

Materials: Various objects that can be counted.

	STEPS					
1	can count objects up to 2	Y/N	Y/N	Y/N	Y/N	Y/N
1g	generalization	Y/N	Y/N	Y/N	Y/N	Y/N
2	can count objects up to 3	Y/N	Y/N	Y/N	Y/N	Y/N
2g	generalization	Y/N	Y/N	Y/N	Y/N	Y/N
3	can count objects up to 4	Y/N	Y/N	Y/N	Y/N	Y/N
3g	generalization	Y/N	Y/N	Y/N	Y/N	Y/N
4	can count objects up to 5	Y/N	Y/N	Y/N	Y/N	Y/N
4g	generalization	Y/N	Y/N	Y/N	Y/N	Y/N
5	can count objects up to 6	Y/N	Y/N	Y/N	Y/N	Y/N
5g	generalization	Y/N	Y/N	Y/N	Y/N	Y/N
6	can count objects up to 7	Y/N	Y/N	Y/N	Y/N	Y/N
6g	generalization	Y/N	Y/N	Y/N	Y/N	Y/N
7	can count objects up to 8	Y/N	Y/N	Y/N	Y/N	Y/N
7g	generalization	Y/N	Y/N	Y/N	Y/N	Y/N
8	can count objects up to 9	Y/N	Y/N	Y/N	Y/N	Y/N
8g	generalization	Y/N	Y/N	Y/N	Y/N	Y/N
9	can count objects up to 10	Y/N	Y/N	Y/N	Y/N	Y/N
9g	generalization	Y/N	Y/N	Y/N	Y/N	Y/N

Child Name: ....

Receptive Identification of Numbers

Teaching Procedure: In a field of 3 or more present the child with the direction "SHOW ME/POINT TO/TOUCH ___ [NAME THE NUMBER]."

Materials: Cards with numbers on them (use different cards for generalization).

	STEPS					
1	1	Y/N	Y/N	Y/N	Y/N	Y/N
1g	generalization	Y/N	Y/N	Y/N	Y/N	Y/N
2	2	Y/N	Y/N	Y/N	Y/N	Y/N
2g	generalization	Y/N	Y/N	Y/N	Y/N	Y/N
3	3	Y/N	Y/N	Y/N	Y/N	Y/N
3g	generalization	Y/N	Y/N	Y/N	Y/N	Y/N
4	4	Y/N	Y/N	Y/N	Y/N	Y/N
4g	generalization	Y/N	Y/N	Y/N	Y/N	Y/N
5	5	Y/N	Y/N	Y/N	Y/N	Y/N
5g	generalization	Y/N	Y/N	Y/N	Y/N	Y/N
6	6	Y/N	Y/N	Y/N	Y/N	Y/N
6g	generalization	Y/N	Y/N	Y/N	Y/N	Y/N
7	7	Y/N	Y/N	Y/N	Y/N	Y/N
7g	generalization	Y/N	Y/N	Y/N	Y/N	Y/N
8	8	Y/N	Y/N	Y/N	Y/N	Y/N
8g	generalization	Y/N	Y/N	Y/N	Y/N	Y/N
9	9	Y/N	Y/N	Y/N	Y/N	Y/N
9g	generalization	Y/N	Y/N	Y/N	Y/N	Y/N

10	10	Y/N	Y/N	Y/N	Y/N	Y/N
10g	generalization	Y/N	Y/N	Y/N	Y/N	Y/N
11	11	Y/N	Y/N	Y/N	Y/N	Y/N
11g	generalization	Y/N	Y/N	Y/N	Y/N	Y/N
12	12	Y/N	Y/N	Y/N	Y/N	Y/N
12g	generalization	Y/N	Y/N	Y/N	Y/N	Y/N
13	13	Y/N	Y/N	Y/N	Y/N	Y/N
13g	generalization	Y/N	Y/N	Y/N	Y/N	Y/N
14	14	Y/N	Y/N	Y/N	Y/N	Y/N
14g	generalization	Y/N	Y/N	Y/N	Y/N	Y/N
15	15	Y/N	Y/N	Y/N	Y/N	Y/N
15g	generalization	Y/N	Y/N	Y/N	Y/N	Y/N
16	16	Y/N	Y/N	Y/N	Y/N	Y/N
16g	generalization	Y/N	Y/N	Y/N	Y/N	Y/N
17	17	Y/N	Y/N	Y/N	Y/N	Y/N
17g	generalization	Y/N	Y/N	Y/N	Y/N	Y/N
18	18	Y/N	Y/N	Y/N	Y/N	Y/N
18g	generalization	Y/N	Y/N	Y/N	Y/N	Y/N
19	19	Y/N	Y/N	Y/N	Y/N	Y/N
19g	generalization	Y/N	Y/N	Y/N	Y/N	Y/N
20	20	Y/N	Y/N	Y/N	Y/N	Y/N
20g	generalization	Y/N	Y/N	Y/N	Y/N	Y/N

Child Name: . . . .

Expressive Identification of Numbers

Teaching Procedure: Hold up the number and ask the child "WHAT NUMBER IS IT?"

Materials: Cards with numbers on them (use different cards for generalization).

	STEPS					
1	1	Y/N	Y/N	Y/N	Y/N	Y/N
1g	generalization	Y/N	Y/N	Y/N	Y/N	Y/N
2	2	Y/N	Y/N	Y/N	Y/N	Y/N
2g	generalization	Y/N	Y/N	Y/N	Y/N	Y/N
3	3	Y/N	Y/N	Y/N	Y/N	Y/N
3g	generalization	Y/N	Y/N	Y/N	Y/N	Y/N
4	4	Y/N	Y/N	Y/N	Y/N	Y/N
4g	generalization	Y/N	Y/N	Y/N	Y/N	Y/N
5	5	Y/N	Y/N	Y/N	Y/N	Y/N
5g	generalization	Y/N	Y/N	Y/N	Y/N	Y/N
6	6	Y/N	Y/N	Y/N	Y/N	Y/N
6g	generalization	Y/N	Y/N	Y/N	Y/N	Y/N
7	7	Y/N	Y/N	Y/N	Y/N	Y/N
7g	generalization	Y/N	Y/N	Y/N	Y/N	Y/N
8	8	Y/N	Y/N	Y/N	Y/N	Y/N
8g	generalization	Y/N	Y/N	Y/N	Y/N	Y/N
9	9	Y/N	Y/N	Y/N	Y/N	Y/N
9g	generalization	Y/N	Y/N	Y/N	Y/N	Y/N

10	10	Y/N	Y/N	Y/N	Y/N	Y/N
10g	generalization	Y/N	Y/N	Y/N	Y/N	Y/N
11	11	Y/N	Y/N	Y/N	Y/N	Y/N
11g	generalization	Y/N	Y/N	Y/N	Y/N	Y/N
12	12	Y/N	Y/N	Y/N	Y/N	Y/N
12g	generalization	Y/N	Y/N	Y/N	Y/N	Y/N
13	13	Y/N	Y/N	Y/N	Y/N	Y/N
13g	generalization	Y/N	Y/N	Y/N	Y/N	Y/N
14	14	Y/N	Y/N	Y/N	Y/N	Y/N
14g	generalization	Y/N	Y/N	Y/N	Y/N	Y/N
15	15	Y/N	Y/N	Y/N	Y/N	Y/N
15g	generalization	Y/N	Y/N	Y/N	Y/N	Y/N
16	16	Y/N	Y/N	Y/N	Y/N	Y/N
16g	generalization	Y/N	Y/N	Y/N	Y/N	Y/N
17	17	Y/N	Y/N	Y/N	Y/N	Y/N
17g	generalization	Y/N	Y/N	Y/N	Y/N	Y/N
18	18	Y/N	Y/N	Y/N	Y/N	Y/N
18g	generalization	Y/N	Y/N	Y/N	Y/N	Y/N
19	19	Y/N	Y/N	Y/N	Y/N	Y/N
19g	generalization	Y/N	Y/N	Y/N	Y/N	Y/N
20	20	Y/N	Y/N	Y/N	Y/N	Y/N
20g	generalization	Y/N	Y/N	Y/N	Y/N	Y/N

References

Baer, D., Wolf, M. and Risley, R. (1968) 'Some current dimensions of applied behavior analysis.' *Journal of Applied Behavior Analysis 1*, 91–97.

Barbera, M. and Rasmussen, T. (2007) *The Verbal Behavior Approach: How to Teach Children with Autism and Related Disorders.* London: Jessica Kingsley Publishers.

Cohen, H., Amerine-Dickens, M. and Smith, T. (2006) 'Early intensive behavioral treatment: Replication of the UCLA Model in a community setting.' *Journal of Developmental and Behavioral Pediatrics 27*, 2, 145–155.

Kearney, A.J. (2008) *Understanding Applied Behavior Analysis: An Introduction to ABA for Parents, Teachers, and Other Professionals.* London: Jessica Kingsley Publishers.

Lovaas, O.I. (1987) 'Behavioral treatment and normal educational and intellectual functioning in young autistic children.' *Journal of Consulting and Clinical Psychology 55*, 3–9.

Newman, B., Reeve, K.F., Reeve, S.A. and Ryan, C.S. (2003) *Behaviorspeak: A Glossary of Terms in Applied Behavior Analysis* (Volume 1). New York: Dove and Orca.

Richman, S. (2000) *Raising a Child with Autism: A Guide to Applied Behavior Analysis for Parents.* London: Jessica Kingsley Publishers.

Sulzer-Azaroff, B. and Mayer, R. (1991) *Behavior Analysis for Lasting Change.* Fort Worth, TX: Holt, Reinhart and Winston, Inc.